IF YOU WANT
GUARANTEES,
BUY A TOASTER

IF YOU WANT GUARANTEES, BUY A TOASTER

Robert M. Hochheiser

WILLIAM MORROW AND COMPANY, INC.
NEW YORK

It is the policy of William Morrow and Company, Inc., and its imprints and affiliates, recognizing the importance of preserving what has been written, to print the books we publish on acid-free paper, and we exert our best efforts to that end.

Library of Congress Cataloging-in-Publication Data

Hochheiser, Robert M., 1936–
    If you want guarantees, buy a toaster / Robert M. Hochheiser.
      p.   cm.
    ISBN 0-688-08923-2
    1. Vocational guidance. 2. Career development. 3. Career changes. I. Title.
    HF5381.H522 1991
    650.14—dc20   91-7426
                                                    CIP

Printed in the United States of America

First Edition

1 2 3 4 5 6 7 8 9 10

BOOK DESIGN BY M&M DESIGNS

Herman M. Hochheiser
March 15, 1906–September 23, 1989

No father ever cared more or shared more

Contents

PREFACE 9

CHAPTER 1 The Facts of Life 11

CHAPTER 2 The Causes of Change 22

CHAPTER 3 Warning Signs 47

CHAPTER 4 First Things First 83

CHAPTER 5 Always Have a Plan B 103

CHAPTER 6 The Shortest Route to Job Security 126

CHAPTER 7 Forcing the Action 161

PREFACE

WHAT DO I know about change? Plenty. Since I began my career, I have reported to twenty-four bosses at ten companies in thirteen industries while living at eleven addresses in five states. In the intervening thirty years, I worked at twelve professions ranging from engineer to marketing executive, teacher, noise-control consultant, career counselor, and writer.

In the last ten years alone, I have been an employee of two companies, free-lanced as a consultant in three specialty fields, authored four books, and founded what is now a growing advertising/technical writing business. It hasn't been unusual for me to be doing several of these things at once, so rather than giving a two-hour speech whenever someone asks what I do for a living, I usually answer by saying, "As little as possible."

Now, don't jump to conclusions. I am *not* difficult to please. No one could possibly be easier to get along with. Just be open and honest with me. Bowing respectfully when I enter the room is appreciated but quite unnecessary and often embarrassing.

My intention here is not to brag, and neither is it to bore you to sleep. You will therefore undoubtedly be happy to hear that this is not the story of my life. The only reason for telling you a little about my past is to show that I know a great deal about change and that, from buyouts to shake-ups, I've seen it all and I've learned the hard way how to deal with it.

That's what this book is all about, that's why you should read it with an open mind, and that's why I wrote it: because I hope that by learning from my experiences, you can avoid traveling the same sort of bumpy career path I spent so much time on.

One aspect of my life that has never changed is that I have had only one wife (why anyone would want more than one is entirely beyond my comprehension) for the past twenty-eight years. Being married to me is no evidence of her sanity, but Eileen is often wiser than I am, and her understanding has been invaluable in allowing me the many hours of privacy one needs to write. In spite of referring to her privately in decidedly less endearing terms during moments of temporary insanity and permanent stupidity, I am happy here to tell the world that she is the greatest and I love her for it. And that will *never* change.

Robert M. Hochheiser
Wesley Hills, New York

CHAPTER 1

THE FACTS OF LIFE

HOW IT FEELS

To SOME people, change feels good. It rids their lives of boredom, stimulates them, and sparks their creative juices. They may purposely get involved in risky, unpredictable ventures because they like living on the edge, seeking out change, challenging it, and getting the best of it on their own terms.

But they are the exception, not the rule. Most people spend a lifetime avoiding change and seeking out sure things. They want to know when and by whom they will be paid next week, next month, and next year. No matter how intelligent and experienced they are, when something comes up that alters their jobs, they'll look at the situation as potentially dangerous. In the extreme, they may get confused and disoriented, even if the changes seem positive. When what happens has negative ramifications, those affected can (and in many cases do) become devastated.

This is what happened to Brian. After fifteen years with the same employer, he had a fabulous job with a decent income, excellent stature within his community and his profession, freedom to make decisions without having everything he did approved in triplicate, and a future that looked ideal. His boss was sensitive, rational, and even-handed. The two of them became good friends as well as a productive team.

It was perfect, too perfect. Amalgamated Dynamics took care of that. They're a big conglomerate whose primary mode of growth is to gobble up other companies. Reeking with excess cash, they bought out the place where Brian worked and immediately proceeded to lop off heads as though they were reenacting the French revolution. Before Brian knew what was happening, his boss was canned like last week's succotash crop.

Brian tried to work with the new boss, only to find out that the guy was a sadistic tyrant who gave every indication of having graduated from a charm school run by Nazis. Instead of being treated as a valued employee who was an integral part of the company, Brian was made to feel like an outsider who was kept on as a necessary evil; required to show the new owners around, but excluded from decisions and stripped of authority. He was pressured into putting in extra hours without pay, brutally criticized for doing the same kind of work for which he had always received praise, and more than once told that he would be replaced if he didn't start doing better work.

It wasn't too long before Brian hated his job, but he needed his paycheck and he was terrified that once the new management team got acclimated, they would send him packing. The situation got so bad that he started applying for jobs with other employers who were placing help-wanted ads to fill jobs like his. Every company he contacted was impressed with his qualifications, but not enough to hire him. None of them offered him anything except best wishes and the hopes that he would soon find a good job elsewhere.

He was frustrated, he felt trapped, and he was mad at himself for having passed up some decent opportunities he had come across over the years. Most of all, he was furious with the owners who sold out to Amalgamated. They walked off with their pockets full of money while leaving him at the mercy of Neanderthals who gave employees the same degree of courtesy and professionalism that civilized people normally extend only to medical waste.

When he got tired of berating past and present bosses, he spent hours coming up with reasons to justify believing that his family, foreign competition, or the idiots in Washington were responsible for his troubles. The Japanese, the Koreans, and the idiots didn't mind his ravings, but his wife did and their marriage was strained.

But just when he thought things couldn't get any worse, they did. As he was getting ready to head home one Friday afternoon, he was told not to bother coming back on Monday. He was given a month's pay, some paperwork on accessing the money he had vested in the pension plan, instructions on applying for unemployment compensation, and fifteen minutes to clear his personal belongings out of the room that was no longer "his" office. He had no second chance, no court of appeals at which he could fight or delay his dismissal, no time to get accustomed to being forced out, and no opportunity to say goodbye to his friends at the office.

Brian wasn't stupid; he could see it coming. Intellectually, it didn't surprise him at all when they let him go. But it was a kick in the gut nevertheless. Emotionally, he wasn't ready for it, and when it finally happened, the pain was excruciating and he didn't know how to handle it.

He hadn't done anything wrong, but in addition to feeling stunned and bitter, he was embarrassed. Why? Because in our society there is a stigma attached to being out of work—that of being a poor provider, an incompetent, a loser in the eyes of one's peers, and a failure. Since he could not answer in a way that made him proud, he hated being asked how things were going or (in the case of strangers) what he did for a living. So he stayed by himself, untalkative at home for hours at a time, and avoiding even his closest friends. This made his frame of mind even worse, however, since it left him with nothing to listen to except his own bellyaching.

Don't judge Brian too harshly. His problem was that he was human. He still is. To say that changes are traumatic to the human psyche would be like telling you Niagara Falls is wet. Career change can be just as much of an emotional shock as losing someone you love or being deceived by someone you trust. No matter how rational some individuals might be when things are going well, spring a surprise change on them and their backbones will turn to jelly as their minds turn to mush.

This isn't fiction, it's a fact of life; thousands of people get stuck in the wake of changes that are not of their own doing. Much of their professional (and, in some instances, personal) identity is tied up in what they do for a living. Their jobs define what they do, where they go every day, how much they get paid, what their status is in the corporate pecking order, who takes orders from them, how much security they have, and what they can expect in the future.

With many people, this adds up to a self-image of who they are and what they are. If you change their jobs appreciably or take their jobs away, they feel like they have nothing left. Rather than acting logically and concentrating on how to get back on track, however, they panic and go to pieces. Typically, they experience a compulsion to feel sorry for themselves, combined with an obsession with figuring out who to blame for the injustices done to them.

Brian's past *and* his future were invested in that job. He always gave his best, always worked as hard as possible, always prided himself on being a loyal member of the corporate team, and always expected his loyalty to be returned in kind. Yet all his loyalty was worth nothing once the company changed hands. That's what hurt Brian, and it would hurt you, too.

The most tragic aspect of Brian's experience is that it was mostly his own fault. Not the takeover or the new boss—he had no control over those things. Had he known more about managing change, on the other hand, he probably could have done something about the crummy way he was treated. He might have even been able to save his job or to hang on so he could leave at a time of his own choosing. If nothing else, however, he *definitely* could have kept himself from falling apart just because his job fell apart.

He got back on track, but it wasn't easy and it wasn't quick.

First, he had to stop thinking emotionally and start thinking logically. His next challenge was to pull himself out of the sea of anger and self-pity he was wallowing in. Then he had to learn the facts of life about career changes *and* about handling difficult bosses. Finally (and this took longest), he had to start measuring himself not by his job title, or even by his job, but by virtue of how much control he had over his career and his life.

CERTAINTIES

To a large extent, Brian's problem was that he had to find out the hard way that job security is a mirage. The only thing you can be certain of about your job is that no matter what it is today, it may be something else tomorrow and nonexistent the day after that.

Benjamin Franklin alluded to this in 1789, when he said that there is nothing certain but death and taxes. He could have given other examples, but he was using poetic license to coin a catchy phrase. You can be just as certain that the sun will continue to rise in the east not the west, that rain will always fall down instead of up, and that we will for all eternity have the honor of being the only species on this earth who were dumb enough to have worn neckties.

More to the point of this book, *change* is also a certainty. Our opinions change with experience and our needs change with age, while the world at large changes with the ebb and flow of political, technological, social, and financial tides. Nothing stays the same forever. The influences in our lives are continuously shifting from one state of affairs to another, and there is no such thing as an absence of change—either at work or in any other aspect of our lives.

In the past forty years alone, for example, a host of changes has occurred in civil rights, women's rights, and East-West relations. The tranquility of the fifties was replaced by the chaos of the sixties and eventually by the greed of the eighties. An onslaught of engineering advances has created new products and new industries by the dozens. At the same time, problems have sprung up that were either nonexistent or unknown to most of us just a few years earlier, with AIDS, homelessness, drugs, and environmental hazards being some of the more visible examples.

One of the most widespread effects of all this change is that many jobs these days offer painfully little in the way of security. According to United States government statistics

- the median length of job tenure these days is only about four years
- as many as ten million of us become unemployed in any given year, while
- another ten million takes on new occupations during the same time period

Much of this transience has followed from a wave of takeovers, mergers, and restructurings that has struck the corporate world in recent years. *Leveraged buyout, greenmail,* and *white knight,* became the terminology of choice for the trendy set, and we learned that there is nothing at all warmhearted about a "tender" offer.

According to *Mergers & Acquisitions* magazine's database of deals for $1 million or more, roughly thirty thousand companies were bought out during the past decade, at a total price tag of $1.1 trillion. I'd like to tell you that all this money led to a better life for all concerned, but quite the opposite is true.

Each time the typical corporate takeover or merger occurs, tons of money is borrowed to pull off the deal. Lots of people go into debt up to their pupicks. If they don't succeed, they go under and most of (if not all) their employees go to the unemployment office. In an attempt to save money and minimize such unpleasantries, departments are consolidated, jobs are combined, and some jobs are eliminated. The same happens when companies reorganize to fight off a buyer or to deal with economic or competitive pressures.

In any of these situations, some people get fired, some leave of their own accord for what they think are greener pastures, and some put everything on hold until they figure out what to do. More importantly, some profit from the experience, and some lose.

DOMINOES

Several of the leading Wall Street watchers are now claiming that the takeover mania that dominated the eighties is changing to an environment of somewhat greater stability accompanied by somewhat slower growth. Perhaps they are right, but even an absence of buyouts will not eliminate changes in the workplace.

Right this minute, chances are that something is taking place that will significantly change your career. You probably don't know the people who are behind it, and it would be sheer coincidence if they knew you, but the changes they represent will occur anyway. Possibilities here include:

- An obscure professor from a college you never heard of dreams up a new widget that enables your job to be done faster and more economically by a computer.
- A company you've never heard of introduces a gizmo that does away with the need for the business into which you have just sunk your life savings;
- The corporation you are with becomes history as one of your competitors takes away your biggest customers, buys up your lines of supply, and drives profits down in a price war;
- The economy takes a nosedive, in which case your stocks are instantly worth only half as much as their value of only two months ago.

Too drastic to be typical? I didn't dream these up; in one form or another, to one person or another, they happen every day. If mundane is what you want, however, the list gets longer and longer:

- Somebody dies, leaves, gets promoted, or transfers, leaving a big void in the chain of command and creating a political donnybrook as would-be successors jockey for visibility and power.
- Office politics at work behind your back ruins your image in the eyes of management.
- A new employee is sharper and more experienced than you are, sending your chances for promotion right down the tubes.
- You're not looking to change jobs, but someone else needs a person with your talents and you get an offer too good to turn down.

None of this happens all at once. Changes in the corporate world are like earthquakes; they are invariably followed by a series of aftershocks, some of which may occur months after the initial upheaval. To show you how the process works, let me tell you what happened to Ralph, one of my most valued clients. Ralph was never involved in anything that seismologists took note of, but that's because their instruments look for shifts in the earth's structure. Had they tried to detect shifts in the power structure where Ralph worked, however, their readings would have been more than the Richter scale could handle.

Second-in-command of the marketing department, Ralph had been with the firm for years. He hoped to move up a notch and run the whole show, but much to his surprise a few years ago, his boss was sacked after losing an argument with the company president. Instead of getting the promotion he wanted, Ralph could do no better than stand on the sidelines and fume while someone from the outside was recruited to fill the opening.

Within weeks, Ralph concluded that in the new scheme of things, he would be either pink-slipped or stuck where he was. Neither fate was to his liking, so he found and accepted another job. That was the first of several jarring experiences that pummeled me in rapid succession. The second was meeting Ralph's replacement, another outsider who was new to the company. She said I did good work but that my specialty was also her specialty, so as soon as she was able to hire an assistant to help her in other areas, the company would no longer require my services. I hoped Ralph could soften the blow by throwing some business my way, but the third jolt to hit me was finding out that his new employer did everything in-house. That company also had no need for me.

By that time, the casualty count was increasing rapidly. I lost a big chunk of business, the same happened to several other vendors Ralph had been using, and at least six people changed or lost their jobs:

- Ralph's previous boss
- Ralph
- Ralph's new boss
- Ralph's replacement
- Ralph's replacement's replacement at the company where Ralph's replacement used to work
- the person Ralph replaced after changing jobs

Don't go away; the commotion didn't stop there. Losing Ralph as a client reduced my income substantially, so I aggressively went after some new accounts, finding several companies that were willing to give me a try. In each case, my arrival changed the workload of the employee or consultant who otherwise would have taken care of the jobs assigned to me.

Six months later, Ralph's old boss finally connected again, this time with an even bigger company and this time as president. What's the first thing he did? He hired Ralph as marketing VP. And what's the first thing Ralph did? I don't know. But he was there only a few days when he called with the good news that he once again had plenty of work for me.

By that time, dozens of people had been affected. A handful of executive recruiters and employment agencies emerged as winners. So did a couple of lawyers who got in the act when one individual claimed he was "wrongfully" dismissed in the wake of what happened. Ralph and I came out of it okay, but others we've never met were no doubt hurt substantially. The irony of it all is that their careers or businesses were disrupted simply because two men *they* never met (Ralph's boss and the guy who fired him and started the whole mess) couldn't get along.

SPECTATORS CAN WATCH, BUT ONLY PARTICIPANTS CAN WIN

There are *four* bottom lines about change. One that we've covered so far is that change at the workplace is inevitable. You may change jobs, employers, or both as often as you change underwear, but much of what happens to you may start out as being neither planned nor voluntary. No matter what you do or where you work, your career is in the same place as everyone else's—the state of flux.

The second bottom line—the one that Brian and Ralph ran up against—is that if you allow yourself to get caught unprepared, the changes imposed on you by others can easily stall, derail, or wreck your career.

The third bottom line is that all changes are not bad, and all surprises are not potentially harmful just because you don't immediately understand what they mean now or may mean in the future. To the same extent that change can rob you of access to situations you like, it can also provide you with the opportunity to cut loose from those you do *not* like.

Is your job providing you with everything you could realistically ask for? Tell me it is, and I won't believe you. Tell me it isn't, on the other hand, and I'll tell you that change is the only thing that will allow you to get whatever you don't have now but still want.

The best news is that there is a fourth bottom line, which is that you do *not* have to sit in place like a bump on a log and wait for the winds of change to blow. Neither do you have to take it on the chin when they blow in a direction unfavorable to you. If you know what to look for, you can usually figure out how to benefit from change. And when the rest of the world is bringing about changes you might not like, you can *always* create some compensating changes of your own.

This does not mean moving on to other pastures every time someone puts a roadblock in your career path. That may be necessary on occasion, but it isn't always easy. It might require you to relocate, and another job may not come your way overnight. What happens in the interim and what will you do if the grass at the new location really isn't greener—move again? There are only so many places you can go, and none of them is far enough away to hide you from change. You may never have job satisfaction or a sense of stability in your life if all you do is to pick up and take off at the first sign of a turn of events you don't immediately like or understand.

There are three basic approaches for making sure you come out on top in your encounters with change:

1. **Make it** and get the jump on those individuals who would otherwise get the jump on you by making their own changes.
2. **Fake it** and finesse your way right by the fools who are more interested in form and fashion than they are in substance.
3. **Take it in stride** by planning ahead and being as prepared as possible to deal with the changes most likely to be imposed on you by others.

Look closely at the people who consistently get ahead in their careers and you'll see that the secret to their success is that they excel at managing change. Why not join them? Instead of being the victim of change and making believe it can't hurt you, you must learn to understand it, accept it, grab it by the throat, and force it to work in your favor.

You're about to find out how.

CHAPTER 2

THE CAUSES OF CHANGE

PEOPLE, NOT THINGS

ONLY IF you know why (and under which conditions) a particular change occurs can you determine when it may happen next, what steps to take to defend against it, and how to make it work to your advantage. Your thinking about the nature and causes of change, however, has probably been clouded by misconceptions. This chapter will set the record straight on a stack of myths about change you've always thought were true but aren't.

Let's start with the belief that corporate change is caused by stock-market fluctuations, oil gluts, crop failures, wars, natural disasters, bad weather, bad laws, or recessions. Not true. Also not at fault are government red tape, stock exchanges, new technologies, the company that employs you, or the companies it competes with. All these things figure into the factors that lead to change, but they are not the causes of change.

Businesses have neither a desire nor an ability to make changes. This is because they have no desires or abilities of any kind. They also have no interest in adapting to what's going on around them, no need to be successful, and no other needs or interests. Shareholders, managers, and employees may suffer if profits are few and far between, but a business by itself will feel no pain and take no corrective action; it can't. *A business cannot do or feel anything on its own; it can act only if and when its managers command it to act.*

In this regard, *people* cause changes in businesses and careers, not things. A corporation is nothing more than a thing that stockholders, managers, and other employees use to achieve their goals, while profits are other things they use to measure how well they are or are not doing. If ambitious people don't like their progress, they'll take action and make changes until they get the results they want.

The people above you in the hierarchy where you work have the greatest ability to bring about changes that will affect your career. They can force their own changes on you, they can filter or magnify changes that come down from their own bosses, and they can do the same with respect to changes that start in the outside world. How they plan for and react to external changes may be more important than the changes themselves.

If the economy softens, the degree to which your job is in jeopardy has nothing to do with the leading indicators published by the government but everything to do with what your bosses think of you and how well they have been "managing the store." The payroll may require extensive downsizing if it was allowed to get overbloated when sales were strong; but if it was kept lean to begin with, the damage may be minimal. No matter how inept the people at the top are, as long as the business stays afloat and a powerful enough boss is convinced that he needs you at his side, you will be secure even if the rest of the staff is decimated.

What pushes executives to instigate, stop, or deflect changes—the desire to promote corporate success? In some cases, doing a good job *is* what turns them on. Some of them have genuine concern for their stockholders and employees. It would be nice if the common good were the main concern of most bosses, but that's nothing more than another myth.

What *is* their main concern? Themselves. Managers want their jobs to be safe, they want to achieve certain income goals, and they may want to do only a specific type of work under specific conditions. Meeting these personal wants is the highest priority of most bosses—higher than satisfying their subordinates and higher than seeing to the success of the organizations that employ them. Of course they strive to ensure corporate profitability, but only as a means to the end of meeting their personal goals.

I am not saying that bosses as a group are greedier than any other group. None of us are selfless saints. We all have wants, and there would be something wrong with us if we treated our own wants as if they had less priority than whatever our subordinates or employers want.

Bosses aren't the only ones who can change your future. Coworkers, suppliers, and customers are all in a position to do things that are in their self-interest and not yours. Managers have the greatest influence, however, because they are typically more driven, more motivated to meet their goals, more able to make changes on their own authority, and more apt to make waves en route to getting and keeping what they want from you.

The changes instituted by management may work out well for them but not for you. If sales are weak and not enough cash is coming in to meet the needs of your bosses, they may make up the difference by giving you less or by getting rid of you and giving you nothing. You can't avoid being vulnerable to that sort of change. Even if you are in business for yourself, you must respond to the whims of customers, many of whom are probably every bit as self-centered as any boss you've ever had.

If you expect others to put you or the common good before their own good, however, you will make yourself even more vulnerable to the changes they create. Instead of seeing what they do as the normal acts of people who are looking out for themselves, you will see it as a change from the norm, it will take you by surprise, and it will sting.

In the process of protecting their interests, those who create change are motivated by some combination of four factors: fear, ego, wishful thinking, and a chronic inability to be satisfied with things as they are. Every time a change occurs, you'd be perfectly safe to take any odds and bet the ranch that one or more human beings (maybe even you) have been driven to act by at least one of these factors. Figuring out which is which isn't always easy, but you'll never understand change unless you try.

Fear

The Midwest division of an aerospace company was in deep trouble. Its president had been on the job for ten years, and although the business was always profitable, for most of that time its sales were as flat as your Aunt Martha's dining room table. Under pressure from corporate headquarters to generate additional growth, the president recruited and hired Fred Collins as division marketing manager.

Fred did everything in accordance with the highest moral, legal, and ethical standards. He was always the perfect gentleman and he never violated company policies. Most importantly, he established and implemented plans and programs that doubled sales and tripled profits—all in only three years. In January of his fourth year with the company, he was promoted to division vice-president of marketing. The next month, he was given a large bonus and a raise. A month after that, he was given the ax.

Crazy? Not at all. Fred was sacked on grounds that were quite logical. With one exception, you see, Fred did everything right. His only mistake was that he didn't make it a point to share the credit for his successes. Remember—he had achieved incredible growth in three years, but his boss achieved zero growth in ten years. That made Fred a hero, but what did it make his boss? It made him look as if the smartest move he made was to hire Fred. Put yourself in his boss's shoes. He was afraid of being looked upon as expendable if Fred continued to look so good. That's right. I did say "afraid." *Fear* is what did Fred in.

Fear itself is not entirely bad. Used in the right proportion to all other motivations, it keeps us from being rash. But too many bosses have too much fear. Unless it threatens them or their ability to meet their career goals, the status quo is preferable to many of

them because it represents no unknowns, because they have
learned to handle its hassles, or because they don't have the stomach for new risks. When they reach the age beyond which they feel
they couldn't start over again, some have a tendency to perceive
any change as risky and any risk as unacceptable.

It didn't take much in Fred's case. After the corporate board
chairman went on an extended business trip to Europe, he returned to find that Fred "had to" be let go—something to do with
falsifying expense reports. The story was a complete fabrication,
but records were doctored, and Fred was history, as was the adu-
lation he had been receiving.

To be a hero the smart way, do as good a job as you like
but share with your boss the credit for your successes. If you find
no sign of having done so, make such a sign. Fast. A big one.
Maybe even *two* big ones. Better yet, go for a home run and
instead of sharing credit, give it all to the boss.

The rough, tough exterior many executives show us is nothing more than a facade that hides their fears. Some worry about
taxes, costs, competitors, government regulations, the impact of
bad weather on their business, or some new technology they don't
understand. Far from being wise and strong, bosses controlled by
fear are terrified of what the future might bring. Their concept of
daring is to wear a double-breasted suit, and the main objective
in their lives is to stay safe.

Some of them, like the clown that Fred Collins reported to, are
terrified of losing their jobs to imagined usurpers who are potentially likely to impress top management because they are younger,
more aggressive, physically stronger, and therefore better able to
put in the type of long hours that big bosses love to see.

To get on the good side of an insecure boss, position yourself
as the person who can be best relied upon to fight off all the fears
that he or she is most concerned about. You'll see in Chapter 6
how to be seen as an asset instead of as an adversary to be feared.
This is good advice to follow during routine times, but it is absolutely mandatory during the type of turmoil that exists during a
takeover fight, immediately following a merger, or in the midst of
one of those massive reorganizations that companies go through

when their performance stinks and the people at the top don't know what else to do but panic and dream up ways to get themselves off the hook.

Fear-driven managers have several characteristics in common:

- they are unsure of themselves
- they take an instant dislike to subordinates who become heroes
- they know how to get rid of you if your presence in any way makes them feel threatened

How can you tell if an individual is driven by fear? Try the following characteristics on for size:

- **A "bean-counting" management style.** Check the history of virtually any big company and you'll find that it grew because it was founded and headed up by visionary marketers and promoters who could see that sustained growth comes only from creating or harnessing change, not by hiding from it.

Typically, you'll find that the entrepreneurs who built businesses from nothing were willing to risk everything they had to turn their dreams into realities. Check again, however, at what happens after a farsighted founder leaves the scene. What happens is that management control often goes to "bean counters"—nitpickers, such as accountants or lawyers, who keep a close eye on profits, dot every i, and cross every t, but can't see past the ends of their noses.

CPAs and attorneys can be devilishly innovative in activities such as tax filing or litigation. They can also be effective in managing projects in their own specialties. As corporate executives responsible for a myriad of functions and departments, on the other hand, they tend to be the most gutless, unimaginative, and narrow-minded people on earth. Once they take over, their employees get bogged down in a sea of policies, authorization procedures, and paperwork that suffocates thinking and stifles growth.

• **All decisions are made by committee.** No one has the courage to make decisions on his own, so everything is decided by the group as a whole, nothing is accomplished efficiently or economically, and everything takes far longer than it should.

• **Everybody who's anybody is always in meetings.** Managers in some companies are forced to attend an endless series of meetings that are poorly managed, without any regard to how much work is being disrupted and how many key people are made inaccessible when important decisions have to be made.

Why so many meetings? Sometimes they are necessary for communications. Equally (if not more) often, however, a lot of meetings means that a lot of people are afraid to make decisions by themselves.

• **The second-in-command is a loser.** Number one seems sharp enough, but number two is bad news. He acts as if something fell out during his most recent lobotomy; he doesn't command anyone's respect; and the only thing he's good at is running errands for number one.

Not quite. Inept lieutenants serve an extremely valuable function: making their chickenhearted bosses feel safer.* Look at it this way; if your backup is a hack, he won't have the know-how or the guts to undermine you, and no one else in his right mind will rush to push you out while the alternative is a total numbskull. Even if he owns the joint, a head honcho who is lacking in self-confidence might prefer to avoid hiring people who are potentially able to outshine him if he screws up.

---

*Others have suggested that this is the basis on which the current occupant of the White House chose his vice-president, but I prefer to let history make its own judgment.

• **Scaling back is the only solution the bosses use to solve problems.** Every few years, our economy hiccups. Sales go through the floor at the same time that interest rates go through the roof. Management can see that profits are way down, and they cut back on costs to avoid going broke. Aren't they smart?

Maybe. And then maybe not. Maybe they're just scared witless. There are several ways to take care of slow sales. One is spend more money to stimulate business, another is to find and eliminate all waste, and a third is to reduce costs.

Many bosses never take any other option but the last. Even if they have the money, all they do is to cut back when problems arise. They look at the bottom line, they see unsatisfactory profits, and they call all motion—good or bad—to a halt. Instead of finding the root causes of their difficulties, they spend their time and energies marching in place or continuously retreating until they finally back over the edge of a cliff.

Of course, one must make intelligent choices when sales slow down, but people motivated by fear don't know the difference between prudence and cowardice. They are likely to cut back not only on programs but on staff as well. They may save a few bucks in the short run, but they'll spend more in the long run, when things change for the better and they have to hire and train replacements for the people they laid off or fired earlier. If they cut back on advertising, their costs will rise even further. The buying public has a short memory, and if a business hasn't done any promoting recently, its managers will have to spend a fortune to remind the world who their company is and what it does.

Changes caused by fear can occur not only because of a real problem with the economy or even with the company involved but by an *imagined* problem that exists solely in the mind of a frightened executive. If that executive has an influential position with a big company, an entire industry or even several industries may follow suit. Before anyone knows it, panic sets in and the hiccup becomes a major eruption. And don't think this hasn't happened. Mass hysteria without solid grounds has started many an economic crisis.

A great many bosses are motivated *not* by the fear of missing out on opportunities for growth and profit but by the fear of making a mistake and getting into trouble. Can you believe that such spineless fools are looked upon as leaders? Be careful not to follow them too closely; you may get trampled when they turn tail and run at the first sign of a problem.

Ego

Your ego is that part of your mind that thinks of you as the center of the universe, able to do whatever you want to do whenever you want to do it. The more powerful your ego, the less likely you are to back down when obstacles get in your way.

That's good. None of us would get far without the self-confidence provided by a healthy ego. An ego too big for your britches, so to speak, is quite another story. Aside from causing you to be become obnoxious, if not insufferable in the eyes of others, a big ego can blind you to reality.

In many ways, ego is the opposite of fear. Too much of either, and you are quite likely to self destruct. To the same degree that an excess of fear can be paralyzing, an excess of ego can cause you to be reckless to the point where, for all intents and purposes, your abundance of guts will be matched only by your absence of brains.

Egotists think the world of themselves and they take what they want, often out of the hands of others who are less driven. Successive achievements propel them to new heights. The more they do, the more they want to do, and the more they become convinced that they can do. They establish increasingly difficult objectives, typically becoming so convinced of their infallibility that they get careless when they should be getting cautious. They generally don't see the need to think about what they will do if what they want to do doesn't work. At one point or another, however, reality will catch up with them, they'll go too far, and they'll fall—hard.

This is what happened to Dan Monroe. On the wall in Dan's office used to hang a sign saying:

> ***May peace and harmony reign here forever***
> ***Agree with me immediately or get out!***

This was no joke. If arrogance were measured in financial terms, Dan could have bought Fort Knox. He would butter up his bosses to their faces and bad-mouth them behind their backs. Unless you had a position of power, on the other hand, he didn't want to talk to you, be seen with you, or do you any favors. Were you to have asked him back then if he knew what time it was, he would have given you his watch if you had a position of power above his own. Otherwise, he would have said, "Yes," and walked away.

Dan felt that no one else was as good as he was. He viewed the men he worked with as jerks, the women as airhead bimbos. Maybe some of them were, but what Dan couldn't get through his thick skull was that he did not have a monopoly on intelligence. More to the point of change, however, he also failed to realize that different individuals mature and develop at different rates. No one stays the same, and the yutz down the hall from you who doesn't seem to know his navel from a hole in the ground may grow up, wise up, and move up to a responsible job twenty years from now. So who treats said yutz as a nonentity who isn't worth talking to? An even bigger yutz like Dan.

Dan climbed quickly early in his career, but as the years went on, his progress slowed and then stopped: not because he lost any of his talent or ambition, but because he had made too many enemies who resented the way he had treated them in the past. When their careers had progressed to the point at which they had sufficient influence to attract his attention, most of them became quite adept at being out of town or in meetings whenever he called.

Dan never saw the need to improve his people skills, so he never changed his ways. As a result, the pattern of success he established early in his career changed direction and he never did get as far as he wanted to get.

Some of the more typical manifestations of ego problems are:

- **A refusal to respond appropriately to shifts in power.** An assistant controller, Linda Brady survived the merger between her employer and a much larger company, but most of the old bosses were kicked out. To become familiar with the group and its work, her new boss asked to be informed of anticipated budgets at the beginning of each month, consulted in advance on all expenses within the department, and advised immediately of any problems. In addition, Linda and other senior people had to attend a staff meeting every Friday afternoon.

Linda couldn't get out of the meetings, but as far as the rest of the new requirements were concerned, she was openly hostile, acting as if they didn't apply to her. Having enjoyed a great deal of latitude before the merger, she looked at what had happened as an insult. She resented interference from someone who didn't know the needs of her job, and she wasn't of a mind to explain those needs to anyone. The old regime had always praised her work, so she felt she owed the new regime nothing more than what she thought was a good job.

Seeing that Linda clearly preferred things under the old regime and no doubt wanting to prove that bosses are not always heartless, management decided to be magnanimous with Linda. They invited her to join the old regime, on the outside looking in.

Only if you become boss do you get to make the rules. When someone else becomes the boss, you have only two choices: adapt or take a hike.

- **The presumption that everyone else is brain-dead.** For reasons that are explained only by an irrepressible ego, many managers operate under the delusion that they are the only people in the company who can think clearly and that the outside world is characterized by a complete absence of intelligence. The competition? Their R&D engineers are barbarians, and their salespeople couldn't sell umbrellas in a rainstorm. Government inspectors? Wouldn't know an infraction if it bit them.

    People who think like this are frequently shocked to find that they have been outfoxed and outflanked by the "dimwits" they looked down their noses at. The shame of it is that instead of learning from the experience and reorganizing their thinking and planning accordingly, they prefer instead to attribute what happened to someone else's stupidity.

- **The bosses listen only to each other.** You might have many years' experience in your specialty, but that doesn't matter to egocentric bosses; they're in charge, so their thoughts are more valid than yours.

    Unaware (and unconcerned) that they live in an ivory-tower environment one can enter only by telling them what they want to hear, they'll tell you not only how to do your job but exactly what their employees want and precisely what their customers need. Even if they're right part of the time, one or two miscalculations is often all it takes to bring everything crashing down upon them. When that happens (and it sooner or later will), they'll have no idea why.

When change means that what you are doing doesn't work, you are not prepared for it unless your reaction is to assume that you may have miscalculated and that you must change your tactics accordingly. You're not perfect. No one is. You cannot always be aware of people, circumstances, and events that will get in your way without warning. If you think you can, you are mistaken. And you are ripe to be clobbered by changes you don't expect.

A Chronic Inability to Be Satisfied

An unwillingness to accept the status quo is a characteristic we all have to one degree or another. Each of us has built-in drives that push us toward creating change. Specifically, we may get:

- *bored*. What we're doing may be interesting and challenging now, but it may become tiresome, bothersome, or annoying tomorrow. At that point we'll thirst for new challenges and seek them out.
- *impatient* and anxious to get things done faster.
- *fickle*. What pleases us one day will be unacceptable the next.
- *ambitious*. We want bigger jobs, more money, and more status.
- *jealous*. Seeing someone with something we don't have is often enough to drive us to get it for ourselves. Once we have it, however, we may soon find something else to be jealous about.
- *greedy*. The more we get, the more we want; sometimes more than we are emotionally, professionally, or financially able to handle.
- *intolerant* of people, activities, or circumstances that interfere with what we see as necessary to bring about the changes we seek.
- *demanding*. The more we want change, the harder we push to get it, and the higher our expectations are; sometimes so high that we go after goals that are unrealistic, impractical, or impossible.

Without these drives, we would accept whatever fate happens to have in store for us, and we wouldn't even try to improve our lives to the fullest extent of our abilities.

If we are too difficult to please, however, what we want may be well beyond our ability to get it. Or we may get it and then be unable to appreciate it or take advantage of it. That's the way things sometimes are for one particular group I am thinking of. Nothing they do is ever wrong, while your work can never be fast enough, big enough, fancy enough, or profitable enough to please them. They'll tell you that although what you did yesterday was too cheap, slow, small, or plain, what you're coming up with now is too expensive, fast, big, or fancy. Regardless of what you do, they'll find something wrong with it or wrong with you.

In addition to being impossible to satisfy, these people are terrified of getting caught up in changes they didn't expect, don't understand, and can't control. Accordingly, they dread change, on the one hand, while not being able to live without it, on the other. Many of them have hyperactive egos as well as what amounts to an irrational reluctance to take even the slightest risks.

None of this would matter if this group had no influence, but they do. They are none other than the bosses who are in charge of our corporations and institutions. No matter how much they get, they always want more. No wonder change is inevitable—the people who are running things are the most difficult to please as well as being the most likely to be blinded by their egos and crippled by their fears.

Wishful Thinking

Wishful thinking has several positive aspects. One is hope, without which we would give up any effort at the slightest sign of problems. Another is self-confidence. Nothing wrong with that, either, as long as it doesn't get stretched into an overdose of ego or arrogance.

On the downside, we get into trouble when wishful thinking makes us blind to the differences between life as it is and life as we think it should be. When the two are identical we feel comfortable, but as soon as their differences become apparent, we rationalize and conclude that we have been the victims of an "unpredictable" change. The truth in many instances, however, is that nothing has changed but that reality has finally caught up with us. Not recognizing that, we get taken by surprise, often becoming easy prey for corporate vultures who know better than to base their career plans on fantasies.

The following are examples of wishful thinking you can do without:

* **On-the-job excellence will assure you of success.** Do you know what happens if your only strategies to ensure career success are keeping your shoulder to the wheel and your nose to the grindstone? Pain happens; that's what!

Remember Fred Collins, who got squeezed out because he was so good that he became a de facto threat to his boss? Fred found out the hard way that excellence may get you nothing more than a one-way ticket out the door.

So did Rick Sommers. Rick joined a business that was close to bankruptcy when he arrived. Not only did they have no sales to speak of, they had no sales manager. The only person in charge of anything was the owner, whose ideas of impressing customers consisted of giving them nice presents, paying them kickbacks under the table, or buying them the favors of an entrepreneurial member of the opposite sex.

This was not Rick's style, but he did get the company into a new product line that increased sales by a factor of five in less than a year. Business was so good after eighteen months that the factory was too small to handle it all, and the boss decided to pack it in and open up a bigger plant in Arizona, where he had wanted to move since he first visited the Southwest some years earlier.

But Rick never made it to Phoenix. He was fired. Why? Because the boss didn't need him anymore. He had problems before he hired Rick, but by the time of the move, all the problems were solved and the company had more orders than it could handle. If Rick stayed, the result would be more business. That would be fine for Rick, but what would it have meant for the boss? It would have meant a bigger staff, more money spent on salaries, and more time spent in management meetings.

This particular boss didn't want any of that. He already had more money than he needed to take it easy and live the good life. No way was he going to reward Rick or anyone else for messing up his plans with a deluge of additional new business.

A similar experience happened to Sandy Stewart, who was hired to assemble and manage what she was told had to be the finest computer engineering team in the country. For eight months, she handpicked her staff. And when she had them all on board, guess what? She was gonzo within a week. "Now that I have all these good people," her boss said to her with a perfectly straight face, "who needs you?"

In recent years a ridiculous crock of wishful thinking has surfaced about excellence in the workplace. I do not doubt for a minute that everyone *should* strive for excellence in every facet of his or her life. No matter how hard I may try to cut corners, I have never been able to bring myself to turn out any less than my best.

The fly in my ointment is that the business world doesn't always reward people for excellence. Success is often the result of concentration on meeting your own selfish ends, not on doing a good job. Many bosses are concerned only with protecting and enlarging their fiefdoms. Unless your efforts are geared toward taking care of their interests and helping them meet their personal goals, they'll want on-the-job excellence as much as they want leprosy.

What's that you say? Meeting your boss's goals interferes with your ability to meet the goals of the company you both work for? Sorry, but in many job situations the surest way to get kicked out is to threaten an insecure boss by being more excellent than he is. The surest way to get ahead, however, is to have a single-minded focus on getting what you want by finding out what the wonderful folks at the top want, and then by helping them get it.

Any resemblance between that and the company's best interests is strictly coincidental.

We behave naively and do ourselves a disservice when we expect others to care for anyone but themselves. You may work under nice people who would bend over backward to avoid having to put you out of work, but what if something happened and they couldn't meet their own needs without letting you go? You'd be gone in an instant. And as caring for others as you may be, you couldn't afford to be any different were you in charge.

If you want someone to take care of you, look in the mirror. Look anyplace else, and you're in for a long wait and a lot of surprises. If you want to know what you have to do to make your boss less apt to continuously change his mind on you, however, find out what he wants and start by identifying his personal goals, not the goals of the organization he runs.

- **Incompetent managers are easy to outwit.** Don't rush to this conclusion until you have examined all the facts.

    Pay attention to the person, not the results of his or her supposed incompetence. The truly stupid manager is the exception, not the rule. Take a closer look, and you'll find out that many a seemingly idiotic boss is really quite clever and extremely difficult to dislodge.

Try to chart how well your bosses do compared to the organizations they are allegedly in charge of. No matter how strong the evidence may be that an executive has the intellectual prowess of a prune, gauge him against his personal goals. Does he continue to hold on to his job and pull down a hefty salary, perhaps even increasing his income, no matter how much of a mess the company (or department) he's running is in? If he does, he may cause a lot of chaotic changes, but he's no dummy and you'll have to be fast and smart to dislodge or even circumvent him.

Bosses stay in power pretty much the same way politicians stay in power. Look at the state the world is in. Look at the state your state or city is in. Taxes are rocketing into orbit, but no matter how much money we pay to support our various levels of government, things get worse and worse. There's an awful lot of homelessness out there, senior citizens and the poor live under terrible burdens, many people can't afford decent health care, drugs are a murderous menace, higher education is prohibitively expensive, and many of our major urban areas are infested with crime.

These situations are disgraceful in a society as affluent as ours, yet the way elected officials talk when they run for reelection, you'd think we lived in paradise. And in spite of their doing little or nothing to resolve these problems, time after time we allow them back in office, in some cases by whopping majorities. Why? They may be total idiots at running a branch of government, but they are experts at conning the masses and getting reelected. They know that many people vote party lines regardless of who is running, that most simply put the incumbent back in office time and again, and that others vote for good looks and a charismatic personality. A small minority makes its choice solely on the basis of competence.

So it is with successful bosses. They may be a disaster at running a small unit, a division, or an entire business, but they are quite talented at staying in power, keeping their bank accounts nicely stocked, getting promoted, and thriving in an atmosphere in which they get security and everyone else gets change.

• **Management's main objectives are maximum corporate growth and maximum corporate profits.** Management's main objective is to keep its members happy, but they will be allowed to continue indulging themselves only if they keep the stockholders happy.

The shrewd CEO knows that although stockholders want growth and profits, they want safety even more. Yes, the old bugaboo of fear also haunts investors. Many are willing to accept a little less return if they can be confident their sacrifice will result in a lot more safety.

As long as shareowners believe that they are getting the highest return on their investment at the lowest risk, they won't pressure management to change their ways. In response, most high-level bosses are conservative. They avoid rash actions, and make no moves that have the slightest possibility of being chancy.

It's true that in the short run, the more conservative a company is, the safer it is. Safety in the short run, however, often means weakness in the long run. Fewer risks mean that fewer opportunities will be pursued, and fewer opportunities means a greater likelihood of standing pat.

What's wrong with standing pat? Nothing, if you're playing poker, you don't mind tedium, and you have a winning hand. But business is different. Only occasionally do you get winning hands in the corporate world by the luck of the draw. Most of the time you have to go out and fight for those hands. You can't achieve growth in business by standing pat; those who try find that their fortunes decline as others rush in to capitalize on new technologies and shifts in buying preferences. Before long, still others may be rushing in with takeover bids.

Stockholder fears are not the only reason for management conservatism. The other is a mixture of stockholder stupidity and executive fear. In return for their services, some of the top managers get paid a lot of money—far more than they deserve. Others could do the job just as well or even better for much less, a fact well known to the incumbents, who also realize that no one else would be fool enough to pay them what they're getting now.

As long as they *are* getting it, however, they have nothing to gain by instituting the kinds of changes that would lead to greater growth. If anything, changes could be risky and get them into trouble for losing money or driving down stock prices. So they play it safe and milk the corporate coffers as long as they can, which in some cases is decades.

How do they get away with it? It's so simple, it's disgusting! Good con artists never run out of ways to show that they are being safe out of deference to protecting stockholder interests. All it takes is some clever accounting, a little mumbo jumbo with economic forecasts, and a willingness to blame all their mistakes on someone else.

In one instance I know of, the someone else was a sales manager who had been fired a year or two earlier. They said he failed to forecast the need for a new product that somebody else made a bundle on, but the real reason was that he was becoming too insistent that they spend the money necessary to develop that line, and they didn't have the guts to try it.

You want to be a marine guard? An artist's model? Stand pat; you'll be a big hit. In any other field, you may have to move fast just to keep what you have, much less to continue your professional and personal growth.

• **You can expect a fair day's pay for a fair day's work.** In a perfect world, the more you did and the better you did it, the more you would get in return. That's the way things ought to be.

But it usually isn't the way things are. The managers in many organizations don't care how hard you work. Neither are many of them interested in how much you get done. They will give you points only for being loyal, following orders, and doing what you're told no matter what you think of it.

If you disagree with me on this point, the facts are on my side. Most people who work for a living get paid on the basis of how much time they put in, not on how much they do or how well they do it. No wonder so many of them act as if going to work is like going to prison with a furlough every weekend.

What's fair from a company's standpoint may not be fair from your point of view. The question is therefore *not* what is fair in an absolute sense but how much can you get the other guy to pay in return for what you are willing to give of your time and your talents. Strike a bargain you both can live with, and that's what's fair in a practical sense.

What does this have to do with change? Everything. If you want a fair day's pay for a fair day's work, you are going to have to change your ways and do something else other than hope for it. You won't get a fair deal because you are in the right; you'll get a fair deal because you aggressively go after it and because you refuse to settle for anything less.

 • **If at first you don't succeed, you will eventually prevail if you try, try again.** This myth was originally an admonition to be persistent, but it is now too often used as an excuse for being stubborn beyond the bounds of reason.

Of course, you should keep trying if your first attempt is unsuccessful. Go ahead; give it another shot to make sure you didn't commit some dumb mistake the first time around. Beyond that, go back to the proverbial drawing board. When what you're doing isn't working, doing it again without making some changes is the height of stupidity. A poor solution doesn't get better through repetition.

Forget about the way you did things yesterday, earlier today, or even an hour ago. Figure out what you have to do right now, decide how to proceed, and do it! Repeat the process all over again whenever you have to, changing tactics as often and as drastically as conditions dictate.

 • **If it isn't broke, you shouldn't fix it; you would be smart to leave well enough alone; never mess with success; and you'd be making a mistake to fool with a good thing.** These all have the same meaning: If what you're doing is working fine, keep on doing it.

Good advice? Sure, as long as conditions don't change on you. If they do, you will have to adapt accordingly. In time, all conditions change, so those who won't adjust are likely to find themselves in deep trouble.

You can do better than adjusting; you can anticipate. Think ahead. Ask yourself what you would do if this, that, or the other thing changed on you. Set up a contingency plan that you could implement without delay if what you're doing now doesn't work. Then, have a third plan ready in the wings if the second one flops.

- **You would benefit from working like a dog.**
Someone who "works like a dog" is presumed to work exceptionally hard. If you think about it for a moment, however, you'll realize that the expression is a put-on. When's the last time you saw a dog working hard? Dogs don't work; they never do much of anything except eat or sleep.

Contrary to what you may have believed for years, dogs are *not* dumb animals. They are far brighter than we are. In return for occasionally wagging its tail and slobbering over a human's face once in a while, the dog has it made: free room and board, free medical expenses, and loads of time to relax and enjoy life. Dogs *never* get into debt, they pay no taxes, and they neither marry nor divorce, avoiding such niceties as anniversary presents, in-laws, and alimony. And they know better than to get a new coat just because some bozo in Paris or New York proclaims that a new style is in this year.

But I do not believe that humans should behave like animals. That has already been tried with disastrous results in the seedier parts of Los Angeles, Miami, and the Bronx. Nor am I suggesting that a jackass could provide more intellectual stimulation than the baboons you normally hang out with (unless, of course, your usual associates are government bureaucrats or public-school administrators).

The funny thing is that there are those among us who really do want to emulate the canine work ethic. Their hard work is restricted to kissing a certain part of their boss's rear anatomy on a regular basis. One who is naive in the ways of office politics might think that these people sometimes get more out of their jobs than they put in, but this is not the case. Throw a dog an occasional bone and it will be your friend for life. Throw people nothing more than an occasional bone, however, and they can be loyal only by paying an exorbitant price in terms of their integrity and self-respect.

As nice as it might be to work like a dog, are you willing to be treated like one? I'm not.

• **It can't (won't) happen to me; I'm safe.** People who think they are immune to change see no reason to concern themselves with it. Wishful thinking and a lively ego dupe them into letting their guard down. When the unexpected occurs, they are shocked into an awareness of how vulnerable they actually are, with the result that their self-confidence is shaken, if not shattered.

It *can* happen to you, and if you don't think so, don't pay attention, don't take reasonable precautions, and keep on believing that change is something that bothers only other people. Just pardon me if I stand off at a safe distance until reality catches up with you.

Be particularly careful of thinking that change won't hurt you just because your job is still intact several months after a takeover or a top-to-bottom shake-up. Organizations are fluid, the dust from one series of changes may take a year or two to settle, and even though you survived the last time change paid a visit, you had better be ready the next time it arrives. And as I hope you know by now, there *will* be a next time.

• **Don't change horses in midstream.** This is total nonsense. You're not bolted into the saddle. If the nag you're on isn't getting you where you want to go, jump on another one at the earliest opportunity.

Millions of people are stuck in jobs they hate, working for employers they can't stand. But do they look for better jobs? Better employers? No. Why not? In most cases, they do nothing because they are afraid of change. This is what Gene's problem was. He slaved for years in the accounting department of a publishing giant on the East Coast. He couldn't stand the martinet who ran the department, and he wasn't particularly thrilled with the work, but he never bothered to look for anything else. The job was steady, and management was proud of having never had a layoff.

Then they all got laid off at once, when the company suddenly declared bankruptcy. Gene had to make a move, so he aggressively started seeing headhunters, reading the help-wanted ads, and applying for jobs. He took the first offer that came along, but the job stank. Did he learn his lesson and keep on looking? No. At least not until that job fizzled a couple of years afterward. Then he did wise up. Since then, he has had three jobs in the last five years. Each time, he left as soon as he felt he wasn't getting what he wanted, and each time, the move was a change for the better.

Change is not your enemy. Change itself is *never* a problem. The problem is not being in control of change so you can make sure that all it does is help you reach your goals without causing undesirable side effects.

PERSPECTIVES

You don't have to say it. I've heard it before. My views are the most cynical you've ever come across, and no business could survive if all bosses were as incompetent, as selfish, as egocentric, or as afraid of their own shadows as those I have talked about here. You're right. No business could survive if all bosses were that way. But who told you they were all that way? Not me. Many are not, and I'm the first to say so.

But an atrociously large number of them are precisely as I've described them—perhaps not every day in every aspect of what they do, but frequently nevertheless, and maybe even full-time when they are faced with intense pressure.

The best way to deal with people who can force change on you is not to fight them but to be cooperative and do your job as well as you can. Just do it with your eyes open—not blindly, and not out of habit. Don't assume that what is wanted from you is good work. Assume nothing about people except that they will put their own interests before yours. Look at what they do, listen to what they say, and find out what those interests are.

But don't stop there. Bring into play an ancient invention.

It's called the question. How do you use it? You ask it. Not by groveling or demanding but by speaking up in a professional manner. Ask lots of questions. Not in a way that might make you seem stupid, obnoxious, or nosy, but enough to fill in any gaps in what you can tell by observing. Ask enough questions and do enough looking and listening, and you'll start to figure out what the people you work with want for themselves. Then all you have to do is help them get it, as long as the gesture is reciprocated.

Regardless of where you work, what you have going for you as an employee is that no matter how unreasonable or offensive they might be, the generals in the boardroom cannot get what they want without the cooperation of the troops in the mail room and everybody else in between.

Instead of posing what they'll perceive as a threat to their security and making yourself an enemy in their eyes, get your bosses to believe that their own success hinges on having a mutually beneficial working relationship with you. As you will see in Chapter 6, this is neither impossible nor degrading. And it *does* work.

CHAPTER 3
WARNING SIGNS

THE GOTCHA SYNDROME

CHANGE OFTEN gives the impression of being a slam-bang phenomenon that happens all at once. But that's an illusion. A change usually doesn't materialize out of the blue, it evolves—starting with something small and growing until it reaches a crescendo.

After years of working at a job, worrying about our employers, and passing up occasional chances to improve ourselves, for example, many of us have difficulty accepting the fact that the bosses we thought were so wonderful are returning our loyalty by cutting back during hard times and dumping us out the door. This is why change can be so painful—you don't notice it until it hurts you or passes you by and makes you feel as if someone is gloatingly screaming "GOTCHA"—right in your face.

One reason why we are so susceptible to being surprised by change is that not all bosses exhibit a clear excess of fear, ego, greed, or the other motivational forces we discussed in Chapter 2. To protect themselves from being outfoxed, they won't let you get close enough to figure out what controls their thinking. To all but a select few, they will show about as much personality as a tree stump.

Another reason is that several people may be in a position to create changes in your work environment and you may not know which of them to watch. Perhaps the person most likely to make trouble for you is not the boss you report to but someone you rarely see or don't even know, two or three levels higher than you are, in an office a thousand miles away. What do you do under conditions like that—become paranoid and start suspecting that the whole world is out to sneak up on you? That's no solution. Neither is reading something sinister into everything everyone does.

ONE THING LEADS TO ANOTHER

The solution is realizing that even though motivational factors are necessary to understand change, they may not always help in predicting its onset. For that you have to identify the circumstances that bring our motivations out into the open and cause us to act (or fail to act) in a way that results in change. For change to occur, the right motivational *and* circumstantial factors must be present. An insecure boss may never show how driven by fear he can be until a subordinate looks good, a major customer defects to the competition, or sales go down in a weak economy.

To appreciate the importance of circumstances, think of change as a chain of events in which one thing has a habit of leading to another. Each event in the chain is not just an occurrence but a situation, a state of affairs. Although scenarios from one case history to the next are never identical, the same situations are time and again harbingers of the same kinds of change. Once you learn to recognize those situations, you may not always know when or why a change will occur, and you might not be able to tell precisely what it will be. In most instances, however, you *will* know that change is coming and it *won't* catch you by surprise.

The first situational signs that many people think of when

they talk about change in the business world are movements in those broadly defined entities called the economy and the stock market. Certain indicators are used by those in the know to detect such movements and to determine whether the economic climate will be conducive to growth and expansion. A protracted slump in the stock market, for example, is often taken as the forerunner to a recession.

Anxious to boost sales, the people who run the financial media would have us believe that keeping track of these indicators is crucial to managing our careers. Are they right? Well, it may be crucial to *their* careers, but I'm not so sure it's all that important to the rest of us.

Of course a recession can hurt, but there's no law that says it must. Your employer may be strong enough and diverse enough to do okay regardless of what happens on Wall Street. And even if the company stumbles and some of the less versatile employees are laid off, *you* may be smart enough and multitalented enough to adapt, take on added responsibilities, hold on to your job, and move ahead as soon as the economy improves again.

If the economy had a rosy outlook, on the other hand, you couldn't be certain that your own outlook was also good. You would draw little satisfaction from a strong stock market if your boss is forced to let you go because the industry you work in is dead.

Yes, you should pay attention to what's going on in the world at large. To know how to structure your investments or to see how business in general will do, you'd be crazy not to check for movement on the Dow or in other influences such as purchasing trends or interest rates. The question with which to concern yourself most, however, is not whether *the* economy will change or even whether your employer's economy will change. Instead, you should focus on whether and how much *your* economy will change.

To do that, you must accurately answer four questions:

- How susceptible is your employer to external pressures?

- How competent are your bosses at managing change?
- How much trouble might be created for you by fellow employees and others whose plans may conflict with yours?
- How competent are *you* at managing change? In addition to being astute at knowing when and how to capitalize on your circumstances, you must have the resources and the will to act accordingly.

As I indicated in Chapter 1, change is like an earthquake followed by a series of aftershocks. No matter where the process begins, be it on the other side of the world or in a conference room across town, you won't be affected unless the tremors get close. This sounds ominous, but it actually works to your advantage, because it means that warning signs usually *will* appear nearby before the roof falls in on you. Just because those signs exist, however, does not mean you will see them in time to take appropriate action. Unless you know what to look for and where you can most likely find it, you may not see a thing.

Start where you work. Not only is that the best place to see signs of warning about changes that will affect you. In many instances it's also the only place where you can do anything to be sure you don't come out on the losing end of those changes. For what do you look? You look for vulnerability—the lack of enough skill, intelligence, or anything else required to stop, delay, control, or take advantage of change.

Vulnerability

Since no one is omnipotent, no one is immune to change. As such, vulnerability exists only in a relative sense; we can't be free of it, but the less we have, the better off we are.

Vulnerability to change can be illustrated in several ways:

- A company that is vulnerable may be too weak to avoid calamities such as a major reorganization, a takeover, or bankruptcy.
- A boss who is vulnerable is unable to protect his or her organization from unwanted changes.
- People who are vulnerable cannot protect themselves from vulnerable companies, vulnerable bosses, and unscrupulous coworkers.
- We are all vulnerable when we are unable to capitalize on changes that would produce positive, desirable results.

A company that is vulnerable to unwanted change is typically weak in sales, profits, product design, reputation, facilities, market research, competitive research, personnel, management skills, or money in the bank. Given the right management know-how and a company's innermost secrets in each of these areas, you would have a good chance of determining if that company is vulnerable to change.

But you may not have access to detailed data such as bookings, profits, or cash-flow statistics. Most employees can't get that information. And even if they did, they might not know what to make of it without a team of experts in accounting, marketing, production, design, and other specialties.

Fortunately, there is another route, and taking it requires neither a calculator nor an MBA. All you have to do is admit that no matter how self-sufficient you may be, you depend on your bosses for your livelihood. The more vulnerable the company is, the more vulnerable they are—and the more vulnerable you are, although not necessarily to the same extent. Applying the same thinking to job changes, you might conclude that a company would be an undesirable place to work because its management (and therefore your security) would be highly vulnerable to change at the first sign of weakness in its business.

What does this mean? It means that the better you are at spotting the presence of vulnerability, the better you will be at anticipating change.

Situational Signs of Vulnerability

Look at each of the following and see whether it reminds you of a situation that has recently happened at work. Don't worry if any of these situations pop up in a sequence different from that shown here. Just note whether any have occurred—alone, before, after, or at the same time as any of the other signs. When we get to the end of the chapter, I'll show you how to figure out what your notes mean.

• **Sales trends are changing.** If you are not able to get sales statistics, try to speak with customers every so often. Ask about their buying intentions. They might clam up if they thought you were after anything confidential, so try something simple, like asking them how they think things look down the road. Another possibility is to ask whether they agree with a recent trade journal or newspaper article on the state of your industry. Some of them will open up to you. Maybe all of them will.

If you don't speak with customers on a routine basis, talk to the customer-service folks and salespeople who do. Next, try the switchboard operators, secretaries, shipping personnel, order entry clerks, and whoever delivers the mail.

Your research may not be terribly scientific, but a consensus here may tell you whether something is in the wind. A downward turn in sales would be unwelcome, but if an upward turn is anticipated, the result could be new opportunities waiting be capitalized upon by whoever tries first.

• **Too much reliance on too few sources of business.** As long as it has several dozen or several hundred customers, a company can survive quite nicely in accordance with the 80–20 rule: 80 percent of the business comes from 20 percent of the customers. If it has only one or two accounts, however, a company doesn't have much of a foundation.

Some firms have a strong reliance on a few large customers. Others depend almost wholly on one market, such as the tourist, defense, or automotive industries. If any of these outfits loses a key customer or if an important market slumps, you can bet sales will plunge and that bosses and owners will cut employees out before they cut themselves out.

• **A falloff in small orders.** Most bosses and sales-people look only at total sales or big orders to gauge how strong the economy is. Both will decline in a recession, but a falloff in small orders is often much more indicative of future negative changes in a company's sales.

The forces at work early in an economic downturn are those of tentative moderation, showing up first as a weakening of demand for replacement parts, custom jobs, products that can be readily obtained later if necessary, and items that could not be used elsewhere if their intended application doesn't pan out.

What's small? That will vary from company to company, but if you have access to sales data, divide it into several order-size ranges, add up the totals in each range, and plot those totals as a function of time. For the largest size range, you'll find that the totals vary all over the place. As you examine smaller and smaller orders, on the other hand, sales in each range will be more and more predictable. In the smallest range, the plot will be flat, with the totals for any given week (or month, depending on what data you have) being essentially the same as the totals for any other week.

When customers start to clamp down on spending at the beginning of a recession, the flatness in little orders will gradually be replaced by a downturn, typically several months before the big orders start to head in the same direction.*

Yes, the place where you work might have only a handful

---

*A steady increase in small orders should also predict the end of a slump, but the upside of an economic cycle often happens more quickly than the typical falloff. When things get better, big orders start to come in again before order-size analysis shows a definite trend.

of customers, in which case analyzing by order size might not mean anything. Or you might be into such big-ticket sales that you don't have many small orders. That's what I was told the first time I tried this technique to predict change. Months before the company president finally listened to me and took corrective action, I told the marketing VP that sales were going to take a nosedive. He thought I was mad. But a year later he was the one who was mad; I was still around to talk about it, while he had long since been fired.

Many companies don't organize their orders by size, but so what? Let *them* get caught in the lurch when they don't see a falloff coming. If you can computerize your sales data so it will show you what's happening according to order-size ranges, do it!

- **Lack of interest in small orders or small customers.** Okay, so you are not one of the privileged few who get to see computer printouts on sales. You can't check against the 80–20 rule, and you have no way of seeing whether the company is experiencing a dropoff in small orders.

Even so, you probably can see how orders are handled and how customers are handled. Management no doubt is very nice to the bigger customers, grandly extending them every consideration. Aside from price discounts that go only with larger orders, do all the other customers get all the courtesy the company can muster?

The danger sign here is treating small customers as if their needs and problems don't matter. Knowing that they *do* matter is what has turned many small customers into big ones. Some managers and salespeople don't know this, so their sales base is static or declining, making them quite vulnerable.

Banks, for example, will do just about anything to make life easy for you if you have big bucks or if you represent big bucks. Otherwise, they don't care in the slightest about you or what you think of them.

The typical bank has six or eight teller stations. I don't

know why they have so many, because most banks seem to have an unwritten policy stipulating that no more than two windows can be open at a time. As soon as you walk in, you see that a long line of customers is already ahead of you. At desks in the back, you also see a dozen managers, assistant managers, and other bank employees who are busy on the telephone, reading reports or talking with one another.

The man at the front of the line has two savings accounts, a checking account, a business account, a vacation club, questions on several of his monthly statements, and a sack full of wrapped coins he wants to trade for paper money. All you have is a check to deposit. Of course you would have used the automatic teller machine, but it is "temporarily out of service."

Forty minutes later, you finally leave. Did any one of the management people in the back have the brains or the incentive to realize that customer satisfaction and productivity would have increased if they pitched in and helped out? Of course not.

Rather than hiring more tellers, banks try to attract customers by spending a fortune to promote their allegedly high interest rates, convenient credit cards, and easy-to-get loans. Some people are attracted to that stuff, but many are not. They want something else that is almost impossible to find at banks: decent service. Most banks don't have evening or weekend hours, most bank machines don't handle all transactions, and some lunch hours are only thirty minutes, barely enough to wolf down a hamburger without choking if you first have to endure the wait at a bank line.

It seems like more and more financial institutions are going under or being taken over every year. Rather than crying about how poorly they are doing, they just might find that a little spent on more service might result in a substantial influx of business.*

---

*I just saw a television news spot about a bank in Japan that tried this. They paid more attention to their customers, they improved their service, and they even changed their hours accordingly. The number of people doing business with that bank proceeded to increase by a factor of four!

Customers might even be willing to subsidize that service by accepting slightly higher bank fees and maybe even slightly lower interest rates, in which case a bank would have a great deal more money to work with at little or no increase in operating expenses.

Banks never seem to realize that although we put in or take out only a few dollars or a few hundred dollars as individuals, we may work in responsible positions for companies with much greater financial resources. They also apparently aren't concerned that we may have other resources of our own that we currently stash elsewhere. If it were more convenient to do business with, I'd love to use the bank right down the street from me, for my savings and checking accounts, but I'll be damned if I'm going to take up sick leave and unused vacation time just to deposit a check and take some cash out every so often.

Then again, that's logic—and not everybody is guided by logic. For banks (and also for many other businesses), service is an idea that is apparently far too logical to consider.

> • **New product breakthroughs.** If a new product is unique and enjoys a large enough success, the company that introduces it will prosper. Its fortunes will change for the better, and as long as sales are strong, its management will be able to expand to meet rising demand.
>
> This is potentially good, because growth means more money to pay valued employees, more security, and more management jobs to handle the added size. In some instances it also means new types of jobs for people who can work with new technologies in areas such as information systems, automated manufacturing, and advanced communications techniques. Take advantage of any of those opportunities, and your situation will probably change for the better.
>
> But maybe the owners don't want to grow. Maybe all they want to do is fatten up the company so they can sell it to someone else with "deep pockets," filled with cash and credit. If that someone else has his own people ready to step in and take over your job, the change you experience may

not be at all to your liking. *You have to observe and ask questions. Only after you know your bosses' goals can you see what they're up to and what it all means to you.*

• **The competition gets tough.** The impact on your career can be significant if a competitor comes out with a new product. Your boss may be forced to make all kinds of changes if another company makes a design breakthrough or just gets aggressive and starts taking customers away from him.

You must try to take advantage of the situation regardless of which company wins. If brand X *is* expanding, perhaps they would pay handsomely for you to change over to their side.

• **Personal gains are out of proportion to organizational gains.** Things are out of whack if a company is doing well and its employees and stockholders are doing poorly. Employees will not produce to the fullest extent of their ability, for example, if they get raises of only 3 percent a year while the company where they work shows profits consistently growing at an annual growth of 10 to 15 percent.

An equally great imbalance would exist if the company's fortunes are down while those of its managers are up. No one expects people to donate their time free of charge and go on welfare just because the companies they run are floundering. No one expects them to fire themselves, either.

A company is vulnerable to being ripped apart at the seams when it is structured in such a way that the bosses can make tons of money no matter how poorly they perform. Such a structure is an invitation to disaster. When people at the top don't produce, they should be tossed out a lot faster than the poor shlubs at the bottom of the heap, who are the least responsible for corporate problems and yet the first to suffer when business is lousy.

- **Unwarranted stock-price increases.** Sales are flat, the R&D department hasn't come up with a new product in years, and nothing else is in the wind. Yet the company's stock is rising. Why? Has the company announced an exciting new product to certain investors but no one else? Perhaps, but then again maybe something more devious is afoot.

Back up a minute. Why was the stock selling so low to begin with? Was the company vulnerable because it was badly managed? Could be. But then again maybe the stock price was low because management wanted it unattractively positioned.

Say we're talking about a company run by a founder who is in his sixties and thinking of retiring. The company's stock is publicly traded, but the boss owns the largest block of shares.

When he took the company public some years ago, the resulting cash infusion allowed the business to grow and him to become rich. Since then, he has gone to great lengths to see to it that the stock has not been seen as a particularly attractive investment. If people in the banking or stock-brokerage businesses contacted him in the early days, they would have been told that nothing new was on the horizon, that sales and profits were steady, and that projections were for more of the same. His annual reports were loaded with facts but nothing that would cause anyone to invest in his business. The reason for this was that once he got the money he wanted from the initial sale of stock, any more would mean that his control would be further diluted.

When the typical entrepreneur decides to retire, however, he isn't about to leave his fortune in the hands of others. So he has his flunkies put out a PR blitz aimed at the financial community. To protect his position and avoid the problems that would accrue if he were suspected of insider trading, he claims that his goal is to sell more stock so the company can expand. His tale is filled with wondrous news about exciting new product developments and interesting new business opportunities. The presentation is slick and convincing, and those who see it cannot help but infer that spectacular growth is just around the corner.

No outright lies are told, so no one is defrauded. As is the case with any sales hype, however, much of what the company says is carefully phrased to put it in the best possible light. When questions are asked later about why things never happened quite as lucratively or as rapidly as expected, all the right answers are ready and waiting to be given. The main point, however, is that after years of seemingly doing nothing, the company positions itself as brimming with breakthroughs.

Handled properly, none of this information reaches the general public. You won't read about it in newspapers or magazines, it won't be on the nightly newscasts, and you certainly won't find it in the employee newsletter. The aim is not to make such a big noise that the press gets nosy but just to motivate a small number of institutional investors and brokers to recommend or buy the company's stock. Sometimes it takes only one big buyer to drive up the price—not a lot, but just enough to add up to a nice sum for he who has a lot to sell.

So before anyone realizes what has happened, the founder unloads his holdings at a higher price than he would have gotten prior to his well-engineered publicity campaign. And since the company foots the whole PR bill under the guise of investor relations, his gain is all profit.

What do you, the other employees, or the rest of the stockholders get out of the deal? Once the chief dumps his shares, the price plummets, so those left behind probably get nothing other than a new leader. Is that bad? You tell me. It might be bad, but maybe the old man peaked years ago and his departure is the best thing to have happened to the company in decades.

- **Morale is down; office politics are up.** You know this is happening when all of a sudden, people who were always cooperative won't do a thing unless they know they'll get the credit for it in the boss's eyes. Your congenial workplace becomes a battle zone in which everyone from the floor sweeper to the general manager has a bad word to say about everyone else. This is particularly likely to happen immediately after a shake-up, when the fearful will panic and imagine the worst.

People can't work well in such an environment. If they were productive earlier, they won't be once the political game-playing starts. Some of the participants may be shown the door if they don't leave under their own steam.

• **The company is having trouble paying its bills.** Organizations rarely make public their financial problems, and day-to-day accounting information is usually hidden from most employees and even from stockholders.

Suppliers and sales reps, on the other hand, are quite likely to say so if they aren't getting paid. And even if management won't tell you that they are low on cash, the accounts-payable people will probably be more open with you, and whoever answers the phones will surely notice an increase in the number of people clamoring about monies owed to them.

• **Job/boss/company mismatches.** Time was when you loved your job and you couldn't wait to get to work every day. Now? Business is as good as ever and no other signs of change are on the horizon, but going to work these days is dreadful. Things have changed and the job is no longer a good match to your needs.

No matter how happy you may be now with your job, you may reach the point where you will no longer be able to live with it. Maybe you'll get bored and no longer be challenged, maybe you'll need more money, and maybe you'll feel you're ready for a move up that you won't get unless you move out. You may not even know why you feel you want a change.

Maybe the magic was never there in the first place.

Perhaps you misjudged the job or the company. No offense, but you may have misjudged yourself and the job may be too much for you. On the other hand, maybe you're okay but your boss is mismatched to his job. He may also be a mismatch to the human race as far as you're concerned, but that's not what I'm getting at and you know it.

A bad mismatch between you and your boss can be difficult to deal with. The problems may not even be your fault: Perhaps you report to someone who is impossible to please. Ego will get in the way of looking at yourself objectively, however, and it may cause you to look so condescendingly at others that in your eyes, no boss could be competent enough to give you orders.

But placing blame won't help you. Neither will expecting the other person to change his or her ways. No matter who is to blame, *you* have to change, and you'd better start soon. If you can't change your ways, you'd better change your job. Otherwise, your performance may suffer, you'll be miserable, and you may find yourself forced out by a boss who dislikes turned-off employees.

• **High turnover of key personnel.** Unless an organization can attract and keep good people, it's doomed. If the head honcho's lieutenants start bailing out in unprecedented numbers, they may know something you don't know. On the other hand, if the boss has a habit of firing key people who do good work, he may be so insecure that stability while working for him is not in the cards.

• **A new boss arrives on the scene.** Say you're reporting to a high-level executive with whom you get along well. Then the guy takes another job, but he says nothing until top management brings in a replacement from another division. The new boss, however, wants his own people in place, people he knows and trusts. If not that, he will definitely want his own management methods in place.

As long as new people can be brought in above you, you are vulnerable to change through no fault of your own.

- **Important jobs are not being filled.** Employees leave, retire, or die but are not replaced. Why? The boss may be trying to save a few bucks, or maybe there aren't any bucks to save. Is cash so short and sales so slim that nothing short of a miracle will save the company?

- **Layers of red tape are added.** Too much bureaucracy and red tape are weaknesses that have destroyed many a large company from within, but nobody can say how much is too much except in hindsight.

  Instead of trying to figure out the meaning of the amount of red tape, look for dramatic *increases* in red tape. If authority to approve expenses suddenly becomes concentrated in the hands of fewer and fewer people, beware. Likewise if things you have been allowed to do on your own authority now require the approval of others.

- **Management cranks up the pressure to cut down the costs.** If the pressure to cut costs gets turned up a couple of notches, someone on high is concerned about profitability. Why? Did something happen, or is something about to happen?

- **Management holds meetings away from the office.** Instead of meeting in the boss's office or the company conference room, management convenes at a nearby hotel to discuss an agenda they won't divulge. They obviously don't want to be overheard. Why not?

- **A stream of strangers is meeting with the boss.** Is there a sudden increase in the number of outsiders visiting your chief? Are they whisked away to meet behind closed doors without being first introduced to anyone else? They could be interested in buying the company, or they could be interviewing for jobs. Not yours, I hope.

• **Personality transplants.** Are high-level people who used to act with confidence now afraid to do anything without all kinds of meetings or approvals? Are the genial ones now sullen and the sullen ones morose? What are they so down about? Conversely, does the boss all of a sudden look as happy as a rooster in the henhouse even though sales have the same profile as a ski jump? Why? Did he just bail out?

• **You have nothing to do.** You used to be busy, but not now. After the most recent reorganization, you have nothing to do. This is a definite sign of impending change; if all you do is take up space, your boss may be reluctant to keep on paying you. You had better do something before you are fired or sent a bill for renting the office you occupy.

Even if the boss doesn't know of your plight, or knows and doesn't care, the tedium will drive you out if it first doesn't drive you crazy. Take advantage of the idle time; you have a phone and a desk, and you may also have word-processing equipment. Look busy, don't let anyone see what you're doing, and send out a pile of job-application letters.

• **No real growth.** The media print numerous stories praising your boss for showing a 15 percent growth in profits over the past two years. What a farce! What they weren't told is that the company increased its prices 19 percent in the same time period. The net result has been a decrease in the number of items sold, not an increase. If the trend holds, the company can continue to grow until it completely disappears.

If you work for a place that issues an annual report to the public, you can see whether it has achieved any real growth. Simply go back at least five years or so and subtract 5 to 10 percent from each year to the next for price inflation.

Little or no increase over the long haul is a sure sign of inherent weakness that cannot continue indefinitely without major changes.

• **The job market has dried up.** Spend some time in your local library. Get out the newspapers from the past few weeks. Do you see much that would be of interest to you? Or is the market for your services pretty much dried up at the present time?

Then get out some older papers; go back few months, maybe even a year. Were the classified sections thicker than they are now—day after day and week after week? You may be able to get some feel for whether things have gotten worse or better than they were.

Don't make your analysis a broad-based economic study. The only jobs that matter here are those that you might want. If you find yourself vulnerable in your current job, the objective is to find out whether now is a good time to make a move to another employer.

You can and should continue looking no matter what you find, but if opportunities on the outside are sparse right now, this may be no time to jump ship. If that's the case, I suggest you make some adjustments so you can make the best of your job until something better comes along. You'll find out how to do that in the next four chapters.

• **Anything else out of the ordinary.** Was a product line dropped? Were any field offices closed? Was a production shift eliminated? Have there been other cutbacks that might indicate that things are slow?

How about signs that management is no longer putting money into the business. Has it decided to hold off on the new roof, the paint job in the factory, or the carpeting in the lobby? Maybe a decision has been made not to replace the company cars this year.

If it's different, a departure from the usual, or unexplained in light of everything your leaders have done in the past, beware. Every one of us operates to some extent out of habit, and when practices change, circumstances may have changed. Look deeper for other signs you may have missed.

It's Nobody's Fault but Their Own

Different people think in different ways, and you may not be able to resist jumping to the unwarranted conclusion that just because he or she does something you don't understand, your boss is in desperate need of a brain transplant. What you have to ask yourself is not whether you disagree with management but if what they did has weakened the company by squandering, diverting, poorly using, or failing to take full advantage of all available resources and opportunities. Each of the following is a clear indication of vulnerability caused by incompetent management.

• **Management expands the business in directions into which it has no business expanding.** Some new products are great, but not necessarily for the companies that introduce them.

A fuel-oil company I know of got into the business of selling kits that can be used to measure the presence of radon gas, a potentially deadly environmental hazard. There definitely is a market for such kits, but not necessarily for a fuel-oil company that thought it could make a killing by hiring an engineer who had a good design idea. Since radon is measured in basements and oil burners are located in basements, they thought the connection was a natural, but the truth was that they didn't think. They had too much ego and not enough fear.

They had no market research; no experience in making, buying, or quality testing their kits; no salespeople who knew anything about radon; no expertise in promoting environmental safety; and no brains. Their residential customers, it turned out, either weren't interested or could buy less expensive kits from others. With their industrial accounts, on the other hand, the people who bought fuel oil were not the same people who decided what to do about environmental matters. To succeed with the new products would have meant cultivating a whole new group of buyers, a task the sales force did not have time to perform.

After being nearly wiped out by their expansion plans, these geniuses finally got bought out—by another company that knew its strength was in the heating-oil field—and nowhere else.

• **A lack of corrective action in times of trouble.** When a company's fortunes have changed, it cannot compensate unless it makes offsetting changes of its own. The problem may be a lack of courage, a lack of wisdom, or an inability on the part of management to recognize and correct problems caused by excessive fear or ego on their part.

Regardless of the reason, the result will be just as damaging if you don't do your own compensating and make your own changes to ensure your ability to get through it all unscathed.

• **An abundance of the wrong actions.** Too many changes are sometimes worse than no changes at all. Change after change that doesn't work may be due to consistently bad judgment, or it may be a sign that the bosses are functioning on the basis of panic instead of reason. An onslaught of mistakes could also mean that even if good ideas are presented to them, the people in charge have outsized egos that prevent them from listening to advice that contradicts their own.

You can spend the rest of your life trying to figure out which of these is at the root of the company's problems. Or you can be pragmatic and conclude that no matter which is at fault, one of them is eventually going to result in a blunder that means big trouble for you.

• **Misplaced priorities.** Some so-called managers have all the best intentions but not always the best judgment. They allow their time to be taken up by whoever screams the loudest rather than who has the most pressing need. Having no sense of relative importance, still others make themselves vulnerable to change by managing nothing, instead allowing themselves to be managed by every little problem that comes along.

To illustrate this point, suppose that quality-control problems are killing business, the sales manager has just resigned, and the new product everybody was waiting for will now be delayed another month. Yet what has the boss just done? He's called you in to discuss the letter the company will send to key customers who are expected to attend an upcoming trade show.

So you spend three hours discussing matters as crucial as whether people should be *kindly* or *cordially* invited to a *wine and cheese party* or a *hospitality cocktail reception*. You ask yourself what asylum this man has escaped from as he drones on and on about minutiae while major problems go unsolved.

This guy is not stupid. He's probably a smart person and a good manager who avoided all the mistakes we've talked about. He may have been so good that, having risen to the top, he has gradually delegated just about all of his own work to others. Alternatively, he may be a she, in middle management, and having just been moved into a job that nobody knew isn't needed.

All these people have the same problem. There's nothing left for them to do but be bosses. What do bosses do? They bark orders, act tough, write memos, and call meetings—that sort of stuff. You might think that's great, but the power-trip routine gets rather boring unless the satisfaction of achievement goes along with it. If a boss has nothing else to do, he may become fearful that others will find out that he serves no necessary function, that his best days are in the past, or that he could lose his job. His ego may force him to prove his worth at all costs.

So he looks for ways to be valuable. He takes command of areas in which no one else seems to be demonstrating any interest. Why is no one interested in those areas? Because those areas don't matter; they're trivial. But that isn't important to him; what's important is being important and he's going to do whatever he can to show that he is.

Another strategy he can use is to start worming his way back into things by looking over the shoulders of subordinates, second-guessing them, and calling meetings for the sole purpose of making sure he is regularly updated on the progress of their work. After that, it's just a short step for him to actually get in their way, pull rank and take back their responsibilities.

Good people don't like wasting their time on nonsense. Neither do they like management interference that accomplishes nothing but to slow things down. Some won't put up with either breach of executive etiquette, and they will leave. Instead of being as productive as they can, those who stay will spend hours keeping the manager up to date, helping him feel important, keeping their minds off the responsibilities they should be addressing, and making the whole company more vulnerable.

• **No plans.** The purpose of planning is to work out solutions to potential problems in advance of anything actually occurring. All organizations should have plans, but many don't. Some managers are afraid that if they used plans, they'd lose control because their subordinates wouldn't have to come to them for guidance on every little question on what to do, when to do it, and how much to spend.

Whenever anything out of the ordinary happens, the employees of a company without plans have no choice but to sit around and wait until the guy who runs the joint figures out what to do and then tells them about it. While he is still thinking, however, the competition may already be hard at work doing what is called for in its plans. Guess which company is most apt to be left behind?

• **No clear goals.** Of course you can't draw up plans if you don't know where you're supposed to go, yet that is precisely the fix many employees find themselves in. They don't know what is expected of them, how their performance will be rated, what it will take to please their bosses, or the basis on which raises will be determined this year.

Is it any wonder that employees working under such circumstances spend their time and effort unproductively? No. Nor is it surprising that they spend company money foolishly or lose their enthusiasm after being rebuked several times for going in the wrong direction without being told what the right direction is.

• **Personnel decisions are based on cronyism or nepotism.** Don't sell a boss short just because he favors certain people. If you were in power, you'd be a fool to give jobs to anyone other than people with whom you could be sure of having a good working relationship.

Putting some hack in office just because he or she is a friend or a relative, on the other hand, is quite another matter. Trouble is often not too far behind when hiring or promotion decisions are made on the basis of any consideration other than who will do at least a passably good job.

• **Too many chiefs.** The company is desperately in need of workers, but it can't find enough with the right skills. At the same time, the place is infested with vice-presidents who are unwilling to do anything they consider beneath persons of their stature. There are so many bosses that lines of authority are unclear, hours are wasted figuring out who is responsible for what, and decisions that should take minutes are more likely to take days. No wonder they're vulnerable.

• **Too many assistants.** The boss doesn't mind delegating, but he's too disorganized to get around to it and he's the only person here with a clearly defined job. Everyone else functions as his assistant, running errands on demand as different situations arise.

Nothing gets done when he is out unless he spends hours writing out instructions so that people are not idle in his absence. Once he's gone and a question comes up, most employees don't know how to answer it, while those who can don't have the incentive to take risks.

• **Grandstanding.** Every once in a while, a hotshot comes along who does everything with a splash, writing memos and calling meetings to make a big issue of what he has done or wants to do. He makes certain that everyone knows about him, particularly the top executives in the company. Agreeing with his ego, his wishful thinking has convinced him that once top management knows how good he is, he will be promoted and his boss will become a memory.

If no objections are raised at the first signs of this behavior and if he has early successes, the person bent on self-aggrandizement will get bolder and bolder. He may arrogantly disregard his boss's instructions on matters over which they disagree, possibly going directly to higher-level bosses for support. He may also take credit for work or ideas that were not his. To reach the top, he's willing to do or say virtually anything. Nobody's going to get in his way.

Nobody else, that is. If he goes too far, underestimates his boss's will to fight, and fails to see the danger of being viewed as a threat, he won't need anyone else; he'll get in his own way and get squashed if not sacked.

What does this have to do with change for anyone else? That depends on how much authority he had before his fall from grace. The last time I witnessed this routine, the person at the center of it was the sales manager. He was cut down and kicked out right in the middle of a staff meeting. Having stomped on the toes of *two* vice-presidents, he had to go. But he was good at his job, and for some months the effects of his leaving were significant—on his subordinates and on the rest of the company as well.

• **A never-ending search to get something for nothing.** The boss who closes sales offices without making alternative arrangements has no business complaining about a drop in business, and one who lets key manufacturing people go should not be shocked when quality or productivity suffers. Yet moves like these are made daily by people who don't understand that you really do get only what you pay for.

• **Management decides to sit on the sidelines, and the competition scores all the touchdowns.** A good example of this is the American automobile industry, which has lost huge amounts of business because its leaders sat on the sidelines for years, doing little more than watching while their overseas competitors offered products that the market perceived as having higher quality and value.

The cause? Seems to me that what happened was brought about by an arrogant attitude that misled the people in Detroit into thinking that they knew it all and couldn't be outdesigned or outhyped. Their second mistake was wishfully thinking that they could sucker the American public into believing the problem was due to trade barriers and low labor costs in the Far East rather than poor planning and bad management in the Midwest. They were also afraid of the risks inherent in doing anything other than what they had been doing since day one.

The result of their strategy has been constant change, rollercoaster earnings, losses in the billions, and the laying off of tens of thousands of employees every few months. If only the high-level executives who might have prevented the chaos were managers in fact rather than just in name.

If asked to respond, I suspect they would point out that running a giant corporation is a difficult job in which decisions have to be made prudently. I agree, but then again they were being well paid for their troubles. If the job was too difficult for them, they should have cleared out before making such a mess of things.

The Over-the-Hill Crowd

Many executives are highly effective bosses at the beginning of their careers, but once they achieve some measure of success, they change their stripes. Instead of striving for continued accomplishment and growth, they strive for nothing but to hold on to what they already have. The courage and competitive spirit that made them successful in the first place becomes little more than a faded memory.

You might think most of the people in this category are long in the tooth and short on the guts, and some are. Too old to do the job or too tired to rock boats anymore, many of them just want to finish out their time without losing anything they have, retire, move south, and leave their problems to someone else. But you don't have to be old to be over the hill. All you need is to have outraced your abilities, and then to be unable to deal with the conflicting fears and ego drives that will fight each other as you try to get back on an even keel. So don't look just for age. Beware of any of the following no matter how antiquated or youthful your boss might be.

- **The boss isn't "hungry" anymore.** You probably face mandatory retirement, at which time management will present you with a watch and a pension. If you're laid off, they'll give you directions to the nearest unemployment office and a check for two weeks' pay.

They give themselves a slightly nicer deal: long-term contracts ensuring that the company will continue to pay them even after they retire,* and "golden parachute" arrangements that guarantee them big severance checks if they are removed from their jobs in a takeover or even an internal shake-up.

These arrangements may be fine for them, but for everyone else they mean vulnerability to change. Consider the mindset of a boss who doesn't have to worry about what happens to him tomorrow. Is he going to boldly manage for maximum growth? Probably not. His future is set unless the company goes under. So instead of trying to make gains, he becomes obsessed with avoiding losses, growth is nonexistent, and the company becomes easy prey for the competition, if not for corporate raiders.

The successful executive is typically a compulsive achiever. When he no longer has any trouble feeding his stomach, he is still driven. But he has no outlet for his drives; he is already a success. So he digresses into feeding his ego. He also becomes consumed with protecting what he has rather than trying to accumulate more. None of this happens instantaneously, but one day there he is, with more money and ego than he knows what to do with, while you're fresh out of cash and on a compensation plan that ties your income to profits or sales increases.

You want growth; he wants to prove he can still hack it. He can't like he used to, but he's afraid to let you do things your way. His way is too conservative to allow you the accomplishments you're after, so the two of you are constantly at odds. Rather than banding together and fighting the competition and

---

*A steady increase in small orders should also predict the end of a slump, but the upside of an economic cycle often happens more quickly than the typical falloff. When things get better, big orders start to come in again before order-size analysis shows a definite trend.

the rigors of the marketplace, you wind up fighting each other and you're both vulnerable.

• **Blabbing on incessantly about "the good old days."** At family get-togethers or school reunions, this expression may have great significance. As applied to careers and businesses, only has-beens think the good days have already occurred.

Imagine yourself reporting to a boss who has bulled his way to the top echelon of the company where you work. He didn't start there; he began as a salesman twenty years earlier. The man isn't incompetent by any means. Sales have grown substantially under his leadership, and he knows the company, its customers, and its rivals.

Unfortunately, however, all he knows now is what was, not what is. His knowledge of the company is current, but the rest of his information is obsolete. He hasn't made a sales call in who knows how long, and he has no firsthand experience with the aggressive competition that has sprung up in the past couple of years. Subordinates are responsible for virtually all of the company's recent accomplishments.

His ego won't let him admit that he should change his ways, and his approach to everything is to continue using the tactics he's always used. That's the problem: A boss who is afraid of new ways will become a paragon of paralysis as fear and ego tug at him relentlessly from opposite directions.

Anyone who has good experiences would be a fool not to benefit from them. But old tactics don't work forever; they need to be updated to reflect changing times, changing customer interests, and changing competitive conditions. In running a business or performing any other job, you can succeed only if you look ahead and prepare yourself for the changes that may yet come. If you look only to the rear while you're trying to move forward, you'll stumble and hurt yourself.

- **A focus on finding scapegoats instead of solutions.** Executives no longer up to their job may refuse to accept the blame for their mistakes, instead citing customers, competitors, inept or dishonest employees, faulty equipment, or crooked suppliers.

Instead of admitting that his leadership leaves something to be desired, a boss may lay blame on subordinates for not being able to pull off his "proven" solutions. Maybe he does this out of fear, and maybe his ego is so strong that he can't bring himself to admit that he is less than perfect, in which case he concludes that somebody else is at fault.

Whatever his motivation, such a boss typically spends no time, effort, or money looking for the real problems. That's why he is the essence of vulnerability: Rather than being in control and taking advantage of change, he'll focus on trivia or personal gain while the real problems fester and eventually stagnate or destroy the company.

- **A bunker mentality.** A boss doesn't have to be over the hill to have a bunker mentality, but the conditions seem to go hand in hand. The signs are easy to see: He'll talk as if every decision has such monumental importance that only he can resolve it, and he will see harmful intentions lurking in the minds and hearts of virtually everyone. Regardless of what skills got him to where he is, he will be good only at pulling his wagons in a circle and protecting himself against dangers that exist primarily in his imagination.

Once a person goes far enough over the hill to rate a bunker mentality, his ego will tell him that his subordinates are idiots, while his fear will say that they are trying to steal from him. Since virtually all of them are nothing more than scapegoats in his twisted mind, he bitterly resists delegating authority to any of them. Power is kept in the hands of only a few trusted henchmen without whose approval nothing gets done.

Why are they trusted and no one else? The only people he'll believe are the people who tell him nothing other than what he wants to hear, while showing him nothing other than what he wishes to see. Anyone with an opposing point of view will be seen as incompetent or an enemy.

Some companies can go on like this for years, but not forever. Invariably, they reach a point beyond which their leaders cannot absorb more growth without becoming a bottleneck that clogs and sometimes bursts, resulting in changes that bring irreparable harm.

Everything the over-the-hill crowd does is geared toward preventing change and maintaining stability. No matter what they do, however, none of these people can make the world stand still. Market trends, customer preferences, and technologies change, and if managers don't adapt accordingly, the organizations they run will sooner or later change for the worse.

The Anatomy of a Takeover

Any one of the signs I've described so far could cause a change in your job. That is not to say that any one of them always *will* cause such a change, only that it could. The bigger and more sweeping the change, however, the more factors can be expected to have caused it, and the more signs will appear for you to see if you know where, how, and what to look for.

Before it can be bought out, for example, a company must have willing buyers and sellers who are either willing to sell, desperate, or incapable of stopping the takeover. This means that two types of vulnerability must be present: organizational, and personal, on the part of the company's owners and managers. To anticipate a takeover or merger, both kinds of vulnerability must be present at the same time.

Owner/management vulnerability can be any of the management vulnerability signs we've looked at.

Incompetence is not the only way by which owners and managers can be susceptible to change. They may also be vulnerable even though they are excellent managers doing an excellent job. How can that be? Simple. Look again at the definition of vulnerability—the inability to stop, delay, control, or take advantage of change. If bosses don't own most of the shares in the companies they manage and if they can't borrow enough to buy a controlling interest, they can be bought out and thrown out, no matter how competent they are. Management talent is not required to engineer their departure; all it takes is money.

Organizational vulnerability may be indicated by declining sales, poor profits, or other signs that a company's ownership is unable or unwilling to fight off losing control. Examples include:

- *The company (or its parent company) needs cash.* It may be anxious to sell assets to pay off debts or to finance recent or projected expansion plans in other areas.

- *It's a good "fit" to other businesses.* Even if it is weak, a company may be desirable if it can help another gain market share or product lines or technology that are closely related to its current businesses.

- *The company has a strong cash position but not so strong that it could fight a takeover.* If a takeover is happening on friendly terms (the current owners and managers like the idea), buyers would of course prefer to buy a company that has lots of cash and a proven record of generating more. If the takeover is hostile, however, lots of cash means that the defenders will be able to buy lots of stock, drive up the price, and make the takeover all that much more expensive. Accordingly, a company may be a target if it has enough cash to make it attractive but not enough to fight a takeover.

How much is just enough or not enough? You can't always tell in advance. Just remember that ownership is not always the objective in a takeover. If the people purchasing a company are willing to provoke a bidding war and sell out after the price rises substantially, they may not mind losing the war if they can buy in at a low price and sell at a much higher price after they "lose."

• *The owners are amenable to selling.* If the people with controlling interest want to retire, go away, or do something else, they are voluntary participants, in which case they may not be vulnerable. Their companies are, however, and so are their employees.

• *Someone buys up an appreciable portion of the company.* A person or organization buying more than 5 percent of a U.S. company must report its actions to the Securities and Exchange Commission within ten days, after which the purchase becomes public knowledge. New shareholders may be making an investment, they may be planning a takeover, or they may expect only to run up the price and then sell.

• *The company being bought has little or no debt.* Nobody wants to buy someone else's bills.

• *The owners and the company are vulnerable, but management is willing to take risks.* Every so often someone with guts says, "I can make this place work and I'm willing to risk everything I have to give it a try." This is often the case when bosses decide to borrow money and buy out the operation they are running.

• *The parts are worth more than the whole.* Real estate, well-established brand names, trademarks, patents, and copyrights can be collectively or individually worth more than the company that owns them. Many a takeover has been completed with dismemberment (not continued operations) in mind. The assets of the acquired company will be sold off one by one, financing the original takeover *and* delivering a handsome profit.

Sometimes, the objective of a takeover is to acquire only certain parts of an organization. In that case, everything else will be put up for sale, with the proceeds used to finance the buyout. Regardless of which part you are with, change is in your future.

• *Self-destructive finances*. To fight off being bought out, to pay for what it has just bought, or to raise funds for a future purchase it has in mind, the board sells division by division until there isn't much left. Or it purchases enough stock to control the company intact, but borrows millions or billions to do it, putting up the corporate assets as collateral.

Debt becomes so high that unless drastic steps are taken, paying it off will eat up profits well into the next century. The only way for the company to survive is for it to be downsized.

Hip, hip, hooray! The company is safe. For now. It may be only a shell of what it once was, but the executives still have their jobs. You? You don't have to worry about their problems anymore; you've been laid off.

Rumors and Denials

Rumors can build up within a company or externally via competitors, customers, or the media. Concerned about potentially harmful effects on morale, management may swing into action with an emphatic repudiation of whatever was being said, accompanied by its version of the truth and a plea to give it your full support.

Listen to the story, but go by the evidence, not just by the words. Unless what you hear is corroborated by several of the other signs identified in this chapter, you should never accept rumors *or* denials as anything but unsubstantiated wishful thinking. So check out the source of any rumors you hear, check out the facts, and draw your own conclusions on as informed a basis as possible. Although rumors often have no foundation in truth, many a chief executive has claimed total ignorance of takeover discussions only to turn around the next day and announce that the deal is done.

A company can grind to a crawl if its grapevine goes into overdrive cranking out allegations about cutbacks or layoffs. If bosses don't keep an ear open for such scuttlebutt and convincingly disprove it, employees will take every opportunity to engage in bull sessions to discuss the latest "facts." This results in the bad news becoming worse and worse with each retelling of the story. Team spirit then disintegrates as the employees, instead of concentrating on their work, shift gears to focus on protecting their jobs. If you have not been through this, I can assure you from personal experience that depressing is a mild way of describing how it feels to work in a company under siege by rumors of impending calamity.

Rather than wasting away the hours gabbing about hearsay with fellow employees who don't have any more facts than you do, look for signs of change *now*. You may not have enough time to take appropriate action if you wait until after you get your information from the rumor mill.

WHAT IT ALL MEANS

By itself, any one of these warning signs may mean nothing. If a sign appears only once, you probably don't have to worry about it. Likewise if it shows up infrequently and then just briefly. When signs are sustained over long periods of time, on the other hand, or if they come in bunches, they may be telling you that major changes are not far off.

Will you always be able to see change before it arrives? No one can guarantee that. If you want guarantees, buy a toaster. All I can do is assure you I haven't dreamt any of this up; these things do happen, and the lessons learned from them lead to three inescapable conclusions:

1. If you go through life asleep at the switch and not on the lookout for danger signs, you are sure to spend your life being the victim of changes made by others, no matter where you work or what you do.

2. The world won't stop and wait for you to get back on your feet if you suddenly find yourself unemployed or miserable because a job you loved has instantly become one you hate or one you no longer have.

3. Sometimes you can stop or prevent changes you don't want and sometimes you can't. But you *can* keep change from blowing you away, possibly turning it to your advantage. If you're smart, you can even create changes that you *do* want.

Don't forget that you are looking for a chain of events, not isolated, unrelated incidents. Big changes are always preceded by smaller, perhaps more subtle signs of the sort I have described here. It's up to you to ferret them out and chain them together in your mind so you can see the sequence in which things are happening. Management will not send you a telegram saying that what it did today may sidetrack your career months from now.

Whatever you do, be careful of concluding that just because your boss did something that appears to be stupid and selfish, it's going to lead right to change. When good performers are fired because their bosses are insecure, the company may be weakened and corporate vulnerability increased. This may mean a lack of security for those of us who are audacious enough to insist on doing our best work, but it may have little effect on the company. New people can be brought on board ad infinitum until they, too, look good enough to discard.

Regardless of which of these signs you see, you have to keep your eyes open to see if any other signs emerge. If whatever happens does *not* result in the company becoming more vulnerable and if it does not lead to opportunities you can capitalize on, a change may have no effect on you, in which case you won't have to worry about it.

This brings us to the most important question of all: How vulnerable are *you* to change? The answer to that depends on how much your plans would be affected by change.

Plans? Those are the schemes you use to meet your goals,

the path you have laid out for yourself as you travel the distance between where you are now and where you'd like to be. What, for example, would you do if you lost your job? Celebrate? Buy a book on résumé writing? Call influential friends who could get you another job? I hope you aren't going to tell me you have no idea what you would do. Being without contingencies is as vulnerable as a person can get.

I'll show you in Chapter 5 how to make effective, useful career plans. But first you must figure out what you want. Before you try to stop change, you had better be sure that stopping it is what you want. Change may be the best and fastest way for you to get a better job or earn more money. In fact, the smartest thing for you to do may be to *force* the right kinds of change at the right times.

But if that's the case, you might be way off the mark unless you know precisely what and where that mark is, as well as exactly when you want to reach it. Which better job *would* you like? How much more money do you need? How many years is it before you'll have two or three children in college at the same time? And what else do you want from your career? Only you can answer these questions. I can help you focus your thinking, however, so let's move on to Chapter 4 and address a condition that's worse than having no plans—having no goals.

CHAPTER 4

FIRST THINGS FIRST

YOUR FIRST LINE OF DEFENSE

DEALING WITH change in the workplace is manageable if you know exactly where you are in relation to where you'd like to be, but most people haven't a clue as to where they want to go with their careers. They move along, rudderless, with the currents of circumstance. Every time someone comes along and blows them off the course they were on, they become disoriented and drift aimlessly, not knowing which way to turn.

There's a word that you should always keep in mind if you aren't sure which way to turn. That word is *goal*—the end result you want in return for your work. Some people target a certain type of job as their career goal, while others are more interested in income level, working conditions, job title, or location. Goals are the first line of defense against change. With them, you'll always know the right direction in times of trouble. Without them, you're a prime candidate for getting lost or sinking in the first squall that comes up.

As long as your goals are well defined and you have an accurate picture of what you have to do to reach them, you'll be less likely to go wrong or even to drift when a change occurs. You may come across detours and diversions now and then, but goals will help you accurately correct your steering if you swerve or show signs of getting lost.

A popular expression in recent years suggests that we go with the flow, but that advice is ridiculous! *Solid waste* goes with the flow: right down the tubes. That's exactly what may happen to your career if you don't have clear goals.

Thinking

If you got the advice most of us were given at one time or another, you were urged to work as hard as possible, to do as good a job as possible, and to refuse to stop fighting for what you want no matter how disheartened you become on any given day. This is the traditional positive-attitude concept, and it's a gross oversimplification.

Perseverance is an admirable trait, but I'm going to disappoint you if you expect me to dredge out the old "Rah, rah—You can do it—Never give up—Sis boom bah" routine. You need a lot more than persistence to set and meet goals in the face of change. What you need is to know that winners do not succeed because they doggedly pursue any old goals. They get what they want because they know what they want, because what they want is right for them, and *then* because they never give up until they succeed. Single-mindedly going after the wrong goals is a waste of time, energy, money, and talent.

What's a right goal? I'll give you a definition, but be careful. What I'm going to say is not without a potentially serious stumbling block; it will require you to partake in an activity at which you may be out of practice: thinking.

You may be able to push yourself to overcome cerebral rustiness, but that isn't the problem. The problem is that in addition to using our heads, we are blessed (or is it damned?) with the ability to think with other parts of our anatomy. At least we act that way. These alternate thinking modes are often called "heartfelt emotions" and "seat of the pants" instincts and intuitions, but I'm going to lump all them all together and refer to them as "gut" feelings.

Gut feelings include the change-causing and often illogical influences we have already discussed: fear, ego, ambition, jealousy, anger, greed, and the drives to escape boredom and take on new challenges. Together or separately, these influences can overwhelm our thinking and reduce it to sheer nonsense. This is why intelligent people look forward to eating foods such as broccoli.

How can a goal be so logical to some of us and so absurd to others? It can because, right or wrong, we rely heavily on gut feelings to decide what we want, and from one person to the next, the impact and nature of those feelings can vary considerably. The people who eat broccoli, for example, do so because they actually like the stuff!

For choosing the right goals, you'll need *all* the ways in which you can think, not just some of them. Common sense alone can't tell you what goals to go after. Unless you are fired up about what you are doing, you won't be able to summon up enough eagerness, desire, and zeal to fight the struggles that lie ahead in a changing world. The only goals you'll pursue are the goals that *do* drive you, the ones you feel in your gut. These feelings are your nature, the essence of what makes you what you are. Fight that nature and you fight yourself, so even if you win, you'll lose.

The news media are frequently telling us stories of men and women who overcame seemingly overwhelming odds to become doctors, build businesses, or achieve high stations in some profession. Most (if not all) of these individuals had at one time been viewed as foolish or wacky for targeting goals that were "obviously" impossible to reach. Fortunately for themselves and also for the rest of us, high achievers do not get their motivation from the approval of others. Nor do they get it from between the ears. They get it from deep in the gut.

Before you can go with your gut, however, you must ask what your gut has in mind, so to speak. How? By using your head as a more than just a display stand for the latest coiffures. Use it for the brain it contains, and call on it for clear thinking that will help to keep your feelings in check.

Your brain can help you make sure that what you feel driven to do makes sense—not for someone else but for you: the person with *your* temperament, *your* needs, *your* fears, and *your* ego. What may be a logical goal for your neighbor may be idiotic for you, and your brain can help you tell the difference. Later on, after you have decided *what* you want to do, you'll need more brain power to figure out *how* you should do it.

About that definition I owe you. For a goal to be right, two criteria must be met:

- you must be compelled to reach it, and
- pursuing it and achieving it must be consistent with your best interests as you define them

If that looks to you as if we're talking about something that is entirely in your own hands, your powers of perception are excellent.

WHAT, HOW, WHEN, HOW MUCH, WHICH KIND, AND WHY

In its infinite wisdom, the state of New York three years ago granted my request for license plates based on the title of my last book. Every so often somebody spots my car and asks what kind of boss allows me to get away with driving a car with plates that say WRK4AJRK. My response never changes: "I work for the biggest jerk in the world; I'm self-employed."

Working for myself isn't a what, it's a how. And it's also an integral part of the way a goal can and should be defined. I hated taking orders from morons just because they were higher than me in the corporate hierarchy, but I always expected *them* to change. I went with my gut, but I did it by being arrogant, not by being smart. I kept on expecting bosses to change their habits to suit me, and they kept on firing me to suit themselves.

I eventually found the kind of work I wanted to do, but I also had to force myself to stop thinking that people were morons simply because they disagreed with me. In addition, I had to change my career goals. I started out wanting to be a chief engineer, but now I want to be successful as a writer and entrepreneur in business for myself. My biggest regret is that it took me twenty-five years to realize that *I* was the one who had to change.

Enough about me. What's your excuse? Are you less interested in *what* you do than you are in *how* you do it? Or is the how even more important? Maybe you have no problem in having limited latitude at work. That's okay. Perhaps you have other considerations that override everything else. Some friends of mine are concerned with what kind of companies they join. One will not work in the defense industry. Another refuses to become part of an organization that has more than about fifty employees; he feels that anything larger is likely to be too cold and have too much politics to suit him.

Your goals have to satisfy only one person: you. But if you can't articulate what you want and you don't know *why* you want something, you may not recognize it when you see it. To shed light on this issue and give your gut a helping hand, use your brain to ask yourself a series of questions:

- What do I want to do?
- What industry do I want to work in?
- How do I want to work?
- Where do I want to work?
- How much money do I want to make?
- When do I want to meet which of my objectives?
- How much office politics will I tolerate?
- How much autonomy do I want?
- Do I prefer working by myself or as a part of a team?
- Do I want to work in a large or small organization?
- How much interference will I tolerate from my bosses?

- Do I want a structured or unstructured environment?
- How far will I commute?
- What sort of people do I want to report to or do business with?
- How do I want to be thought of by others?

Each of these questions represents a gut-feel issue. The answers can be neither right nor wrong as long as they reflect what you feel. If you have difficulty in coming up with answers you like, look again at the questions. Would it be easier for you to answer them if you were asked to indicate the *minimum* you would find acceptable in each case? You can answer with one word, a paragraph, several paragraphs, a number, or a range between two numbers—whatever lets you best express yourself. Give the first response that comes into your mind; you are looking for feelings, not positions that are well thought out.

Aptitude alone is a poor basis on which to plan a career. I've met lots of people who are good at what they do and yet they hate it. What you are good at says nothing about the how, where, when, how much, and what kind of issues play an important role in determining whether you will be satisfied in a given job. All these issues must be dealt with, and the only way you can do that is to be highly specific and ruthlessly inquisitive in setting your goals.

Suppose you feel that your career is going in an unacceptable direction. Ask yourself why you feel that way. What would have to happen to change your mind? Don't say, "I just don't like it," or, "I don't know." Answers like that don't mean anything. Go back to the what, how, when, how much, which kind, and why questions. Ask them of yourself, and come up with some specific answers. Is it money? How much? If you can't put a figure down, how about a range. More latitude? How much more? Write it out.

Don't set goals by saying something as ambiguous as, "I'd like to run a big business." What business? In what industry? Why do you want to run it? Is it power? Prestige? Money? How much? Whatever your reasons, are they enough to make up for the hours and the pressures that you would have to endure?

You may not be able to answer these questions easily, but try anyway. If you don't know why you have chosen one direction over another, you don't know anything.

That's what happened to Sally. She was the vice-president of public relations for a power company that was gobbled up by a bigger power company. She really loved the job, and she was good—damn good, maybe one of the best. But the new management team had its own PR person. Sally wasn't fired after the merger, but bit by bit her responsibilities were taken away until the only thing she had left to do was to resign.

She found another job in less than a month. Taking it forced her to move, but the perks were all there: more money, a company car, and a real staff this time. She had to do almost everything herself on the old job, but now she could finally be an executive and delegate to others.

She hated it: too much managing and not enough doing. So she moved again to another job, and then another. She hated them, too. After three or four years, she concluded that maybe she should be in business for herself as a publicity consultant. That lasted eight months. It wasn't that she couldn't get clients or do good work, but she didn't want the hassle. "I can't survive unless I get paid," she explained, "but I can't do that unless I do work, and I can't do that while I'm out trying to sell myself to new clients."

One day in the midst of writing a promotional story about a tour of an allegedly exotic place she knew was a run-down rat trap, Sally started to make sense out of her troubles. Analyzing what she did for her business as opposed to her work when she was at the power company, she realized that what she enjoyed was selling ideas, not making bad ideas sound good. She also enjoyed dealing on a high level with interesting, intelligent people.

Sally straightened out her career by becoming a lobbyist for an international trade association. No administrative stuff, no late nights at the word processor, and more rejections in a month than you or I will see in a lifetime—but she wouldn't have it any other way.

Even if you think you have what you want, things can change and cause you to lose it. Like Sally, if you don't know *what* you've lost, you're going to have an awful time finding it again.

EXPAND YOUR HORIZONS AND TAP YOUR EXPERIENCES

One of the difficulties with gut feelings is that they react only to what they have experienced. If you have no knowledge of a business or type of work, it doesn't exist as far as your gut is concerned; you have to dream it up or see it in use by someone else. This is why some people don't have goals: They haven't seen anything they like, so nothing has yet inspired them.

None of this would matter if they could use the force of willpower to conjure up goals that interest them, but they can't. You can't, either. Your gut feelings do not speak for themselves. You may have to experience them several times in several ways before you know what they mean, see what does and does not work, and adjust your tactics as you go. This will not happen if you hide in a closet. It happens if you make a conscious effort to expose yourself (no exhibitionist jokes, please) to as broad as possible a spectrum of experiences, and then make the most of them. You have to use your brain as well as your eyes and ears, but it's not all that hard; there are several options you can take:

> • **Educate yourself.** The education I'm talking about is not for the vague purpose of becoming well rounded. Ron was extremely well rounded. At 335 pounds, he couldn't be much of anything else, but taking on the appearance of a one-man fat farm wasn't his only problem. He was thirty years old, but after a series of jobs as a junior accountant he was working hard, going no place, enjoying nothing, and he didn't know what else to do.

At first, all he could think of was that he wanted to make more money. He said he wanted to have so much of it that it would be "coming out of his ears." The way he looked, however, you'd think he wanted it stuffed in his shirt; the guy was so bulbous that his wife threatened to have him arrested for impersonating a whale.

I don't know what woke him up, but Ron finally realized that he needed a *way* to make more money, a *how* to match the *what* that he wanted. To discover that way, he decided to discover more about what the world could offer him. He had gone to college years earlier, but now he wanted to learn. So he went back to school—two evenings a week at first, literature and political science.

This seemed nutty to many of his friends, but Ron had a plan. Since he had no ideas of his own about what he might want to do, his scheme was to see what ideas other people had, the work they did, and why they did it. It took several years, but he poured himself into it and becoming more and more knowledgeable became an obsession to him.

That's still the case today, except now he learns by reading: newspapers, magazines, even the nutritional rundown on the side of cereal boxes. The news is all he watches on TV. But he doesn't take courses anymore; he gives them—as a teacher. "The money stinks," he jokes, "but the working conditions are horrible."

Don't let him kid you. He wouldn't do anything else, and his overall income isn't bad at all. On reflection, he now realizes that although getting rich would still be nice, what he really wanted was to get more satisfaction from his work. Aside from his teaching salary, he still does taxes for a handful of clients. And since going on a diet, he has found that filling his mind is more rewarding than filling his mouth.

Ron wasn't lucky. He didn't fall into anything, and even now he isn't living in paradise. He wanted a sense of liking what he did for a living, and he finally realized that he had to go look for it. He looked nights while he worked days. That isn't luck; it's a grind, a smart grind.

• **Benefit from your mistakes.** In many situations, the best way to learn is to charge right in and try new things, screwing up as need be to get action, figuring out where you went wrong, and correcting your mistakes on your next attempt. Setting career goals is no different; sometimes the only way to find whether a career path suits you is to try it.

Experimenting with careers is not without risk. It could eat up a big chunk of your life and leave you with nothing to show for your efforts. But before you conclude that learning from your mistakes isn't for you, permit me to point out that you probably do it more often than you realize.

Suppose, for example, that you stay in the field you are in now but you change employers. You meet with your new boss before you make the switch, but you won't know until afterward whether conditions were as you thought they would be. Perhaps you will hate it. The new job could be worse than what you expected. Your ability to grow and to advance may be less than what it is now. How do you find out? By giving it a go and getting out if it turns out to be a mistake—that's how. There is no other way.

Trying a few things on for size may be difficult when you have a pile of pressing personal responsibilities hanging over your head, but you may be able to do something new on a free-lance or volunteer basis. Part-time activities are often a great way to examine the ins and outs of a new line of work without taking the complete plunge. Ridiculous? No more so than being grossly underpaid for the rest of your life or slaving away for years at a job you hate. That's insane; what I'm suggesting is merely gutsy. If you can't stomach what you are doing now, the craziest solution is to do nothing. Do something else, go somewhere else, or make some other changes that will get you out of that rut you're in.

• **Dissect what you've done into its smallest elements.** After being out of work for almost sixteen months, Mark was desperately looking for something—anything— that would bring in a few dollars. Having been engineering vice-president before his last employer went bankrupt, he was looking at the fancy job titles section of the help-wanted ads.

His wife, Sandy, had more brains than that. They had no money, and she was looking in what Mark had mistakenly thought of as the crummy job titles section. Someone wanted a part-time programmer. "Haven't you written computer programs?" she asked. "Of course," he replied. And of course he applied and got the job. He has since moved on to bigger and better things, but not in engineering; he is in programming, as a consultant. He never would have thought of going that route that if he hadn't been forced into it, but he's glad he did.

Having waited until his back was to the wall before he sorted out his preferences by accident, maybe Mark was lucky. But you don't have to leave things to chance. Look back at every job you've had. Forget job titles, forget company names, forget the names of the bosses you reported to, and forget what your desk looked like. Most importantly, forget about whether you were fairly compensated for your efforts.

What *should* you do? Treat doing what you want and getting what you want as separate entities. Individually figure out the work you've liked and the rewards you seek. Then determine how to put the two together.

A good way to do this is by emulating Mark and looking at the advertised job openings—all of them, from A to Z. Again, don't look at titles; look at job functions and responsibilities. Rule nothing out; you aren't signing your life away, you are merely searching for reminders of work you have done. To trigger your thinking, listed below are examples of on-the-job tasks that at one time or another may have been a large (or even a small) part of your everyday life:

answer phones	fill out forms	run tests
calculate	fix things	sell
climb	give orders	sit in meetings

collect money	heal	solve problems
communicate	inform others	stack
cook	inspect	take orders
coordinate	lift	take things apart
count	make things run	talk
deliver	operate equipment	teach
dig holes	organize	tell people where to go
draw pictures	put things together	travel from one place
drive a vehicle	read	to another
figure things out	run meetings	type
		write

As you look at this list, remember that what you're trying to do is identify goals that you will continue to pursue no matter what changes are brought about by your employer, the economy, or anything else. If you can think of activities that are not on this list, please add them in.

Then check off those items you particularly enjoyed. When you're done, go back and add a mark to any item you believe you might have enjoyed had you not been restricted one way or another by company policies or your boss's orders. Have you checked or added everything of interest to you? If the only time you did something was one Tuesday afternoon ten years ago but you enjoyed it immensely, put it down and look into its possibilities. When you're done, you may have two items marked or you may have twenty, but at least you will have started the process of finding goals that are right for you.

PRIORITIES

You can't manage change without having solid goals, but I'm sure that you have more than just one career goal. Income level, type of work, a desired level of authority, security, and prestige are among many objectives that you may have staked out for yourself to meet within a framework of various timetables.

Your resources for achieving all these goals, however, are

not without bounds. You have only so much energy, patience, influence, money, time, and wisdom. If you squander what you have in pursuit of what is *not* most important to you, you may not have enough left over to take care of the items you want most.

As a result, you may not be able to get everything you want as soon as you'd like to get it. Some of it you may never get. Some of it may come within reach, but you may turn it down to avoid conflicting with other goals, such as not wanting to relocate.

But this doesn't mean that you must limit yourself to only a few goals. Set as many goals as you like, but recognize that you may not be able to meet all of them simultaneously. You may be able to do no better than achieve them over a period of months or years in a rank-ordered sequence. Such a sequence is commonly known as a priority list, and it is typically based on what you want the most, in conjunction with how much you can pay for your wants with hard work or with anything else that will help.

A priority list is a combination rudder and sonar device that will keep you going directly toward the goals that mean the most to you. The difficulty is that it isn't always easy to decide which goals should be at the top of your list. One gut feel wants you to do this, another wants you to do that, and the two may conflict with one another. That's why tough decisions are called gut-wrenching rather than brain-wrenching.

If you find yourself stuck in the grip of priority selection, perhaps the following tips will help:

• **Go first for the goals that can't wait.** The most important priority you face may change from day to day, depending upon what can be done now as opposed to what can be done later. The next time you face goals that appear to be in conflict, you may *not* have to pick one over the other. Look at what you have before you as a problem of scheduling, not of eliminating. Can any of your options be delayed, while others will disappear if you don't pick them now? Will one cost more in the future while the other won't?

• **Distinguish needs from wants.** Another possibility is to look at goals in conflict as a war of wants versus needs. We use these terms interchangeably in conversation, but to *want* something is to feel a desire for it, while to *need* it is to be at risk without it. You may need a cure for athlete's foot, but you do not want it in your breakfast cereal. Similarly, no matter how much you might want a scotch and soda, you really don't need it.

The reason some businesses fail is that they are run by meatheads who throw money away on status symbols and other garbage they don't need and can't afford. They think they need letterheads and business cards, a good location, furniture, a facsimile/answering machine, and maybe a word processor and a car phone. But they don't need all that crap. They want it. Some of them don't need any of it. What *do* they need? Paying customers.

When choosing between goals to determine which of them more accurately reflects your priorities, ask yourself which of them are needs and which are wants. At the top of your list put those that are both needs *and* wants. At the bottom, place those that are wants only. You may not be able to place every priority in a neat ranking, but when objectives seem to conflict with one another, you should be able to determine whether each of them has a high, medium, or low priority. If you can get that far with a first-cut analysis, look further at the goals in each category. Perhaps you can create even finer distinctions.

• **Do what has the best chance of making you a hero to your boss.** I pointed out in Chapter 2 that the surest way to motivate your bosses to do what you want is to help them get what *they* want. This is often an excellent basis on which to set your priorities.

So there you are, sitting on the horns of dilemma. This

is not a comfortable place to be. Your boss wants you to finish a sales report this afternoon, but you see a better use for your time. You want to go to the manufacturing department to see if you can help figure out why it has been having so many quality-control problems. You decide to tend to the latter problem: It's costing the company a fortune to replace broken parts, but no money is riding on the report, so it will have to wait.

This is a risky decision. There *is* money riding on that report—the amount the company pays you. For all you know, your boss is under the gun from his boss on that report you've been asked for, and both of them are under so much pressure that neither of them cares about quality problems right now.

To make the right choice, ask yourself what *your* bottom-line goal is in all this—not the company's goal, *your* goal. If your aim is to further your career and enhance your income, do what your boss asks when a conflict arises. You could spell out the details and let the boss pick, but don't be surprised if his choice is that you stick around after hours so you can do what you want *and* what he wants.

Can you stay late and not interfere with some other priority of yours? If not, maybe you should just do what the boss asks of you, make yourself a hero in his eyes, and be done with it at that.

• **Compare penalties.** The other day a friend of mine said that she missed out on something because she *had to* go out of town on business. When she got back, she apologized for not being able to meet with me for a couple of days on a project we were working on. "I *have to* catch up on my work today," she said. "And tomorrow I *must* prepare for next week's planning meetings."

I wouldn't begin to question her judgment, but I can't help conjuring up images of what people mean by *had to*, *have to*, or *must*. They are such familiar expressions. They bring up images of doing one thing to avoid something else that is extremely unpleasant. The next time you think that you "have to" attack one goal as opposed to another, try playing a little game. I call it What's the Penalty?

Your greatest need is the goal that will result in the most horrible penalty if you do not achieve it. That's the goal that will cause you the most pain if you never reach it and the goal to which all others must take a backseat—the goal at the top of your priority list.

What terrible fate would happen if you didn't do what you think you *have to* do? Would you be forcibly separated from your fingernails? Condemned to spend the rest of your life watching dog food commercials? Probably not, but what *would* happen? Examining the actual severity of the penalty can put your needs and wants in their true perspective. Also known as worst-case analysis, comparison of penalties is particularly useful if one of the options in front of you is to stand pat and do nothing.

Some of these schemes may be long shots in terms of helping to establish your priorities. Maybe all of them are, but I doubt it. If you can look at yourself and your goals objectively, these schemes *can* work, they cost nothing, and the payoffs are enormous when they do work. They're worth trying no matter what the odds.

You have to try them. *Have to?* That's right, a crushing penalty may be imposed on you if you have no priorities. The people who are most likely to inflict change on you won't hesitate at all if they think you represent a danger to them. They may be wrong, but they are single-minded, they are ruthless, they never have difficulty sorting out their priorities, and they'll get rid of you any way they can, as fast as they can. You'll see the result as change, but they'll see it as nothing more than eliminating an obstacle.

To achieve your own goals with minimum interference from change, you will need all the focus you can get. You cannot possibly get your way if you don't know which way you prefer the most. Yet that is precisely what will happen if rather than decisively taking the right actions at the right times, you get sidetracked by arguing with yourself about which of your goals to pursue.

REALISM

Suppose your career goal was to perfect the safe use of nitroglycerin in a fast-acting dental floss. Okay, so it's *very* fast acting. You undoubtedly know numerous business associates and former bosses on whom you'd like to experiment with such a product, but forget it; this goal is not realistic.

I know; neither is that example. But it does show that going with your gut should not be taken as a license to indulge in sophomoric fantasies. So let's get closer to home and see what you would do in a more typical career situation.

Think of yourself as being the sales manager for a small electronic-components manufacturer located in suburban Baltimore. The bulk of your customer base is in Dallas, Des Moines, Orlando, Boston, and various spots up and down the California coastline. You make an excellent income and your job is certainly secure, but after ten years on the road, you've had it. You're tired of traveling, tired of living out of a suitcase, tired of not being able to be home more often, tired of eating mostly in restaurants, and tired of running from one plane to another and one city to another.

In looking around for alternatives you remember an ambition from years past: to work as a landscape architect. You love plants, and before you took on this current job, you were quite good at laying out gardens and floral displays. You would love to do that now in your spare time, but you can never predict when that will be, so you don't even bother.

In a conversation with an old friend you haven't seen in years, you find that he/she is in the landscaping business and would love you to come in with her/him. The drawbacks are that you'd have to start out at less than a third of your current salary and to go to night school to gain some important knowledge you don't have. The school thing would be short-term, but your income might take years to get back to where it was. You'd like nothing better than to give it a shot, but wouldn't the whole idea be unrealistic?

Don't answer that question. I haven't given you enough information. If you have no family to support in this hypothetical scenario, it might be realistic to try going in with your friend for a couple of years, particularly if you have enough assets to tide you over through the rough spots. But what if you *do* have a family? How about four children in college at the same time? A drastic income reduction would be most unrealistic, and you would be well advised to postpone your plans until the kids have graduated.

Even then, maybe you could get a sabbatical from your job to try out the new situation. Perhaps you can do the landscaping bit part-time, take a local sales job part-time to augment your income, and make a smooth transition instead of jumping into another profession all at once.

Another fact I haven't told you is where the new opportunity is. If you didn't have to relocate, at least you might know some people you could rely on if things don't pan out. But what would you do if the the new situation is halfway across the country, where other jobs are scarce or nonexistent? Would that be more of a risk than you could accept? Even if you are happy in your new career, your family might be miserable in their new surroundings. Any move can be stressful when it puts people in a different environment. Are you being unrealistic in assuming that life would be a bed of roses just because you would be leaving that job you hate? Or have you forgotten that a bed of roses may be full of thorns?

I could go on, but you're probably getting the message by now. Nothing to do with reality in goal setting is black or white. Everything about it is one shade of gray or another, and the best you can do is come up with a shade you like in context with your priorities, resources, and circumstances. Thus constrained, a goal can be called realistic if it meets three criteria:

- you want it
- you can get it without divine intervention
- if you fail, you will be able to recover, perhaps learning enough from the experience to make a more successful try later

This is of another way of defining what a right goal is, but as you can see, it has nothing to do with ease of accomplishment. What is realistic may be incredibly difficult. Nor does it necessarily mean fast. Some realistic goals can be accomplished quickly, while others may take years.

Many people let themselves be governed by fear. When they conclude that a goal is realistic even though reaching it would expose them to great danger, they may want that goal so much that the fear of not getting it is all-consuming. They may do nothing, however, if they are controlled by the fear of running into trouble by not playing it safe. Whichever one of these fears dominates, they will lean in one direction or another, rationalizing their choice to sound as if it were logical when in fact logic had nothing to do with it.

To avoid falling into the fears trap without a fight, separate what you want from how you can best achieve it. You may not always be able to get everything on your wish list, but many a wild idea can be made realistic if you force the issue with the right methodology.

So don't just stop and give up if you suspect that a career goal is unrealistic. Analyze the situation. Ask yourself *why* you feel that way. Can you improve or modify your circumstances? Add to your resources? Alter your goals without giving up on them? Don't rest until you figure out what is missing that would provide more realism.

But if you can't bring yourself to bite the bullet and do everything you should do to meet a goal, figure out what you *can* do, and do that. When your problem is an itch caused by a bug on the bottom of your foot, don't just cogitate; stomp on it or at least flick it away. The itch won't disappear if you do nothing other than sit there like a dummy and scratch your head while you pick your nose.

I am not saying that you should take rash actions, but you must take *some* actions. Rather than going for everything in one gulp, you might feel better if you divided your goals into a sequence of smaller steps, assigned a priority to each, and marshaled your resources accordingly. Perhaps you would be more at ease with your goals if you thought of meeting them in two years instead of one; doing some of what has to be done now, and some later—after you have saved, earned, or borrowed more cash.

This is called planning, and it is the best way to put your objectives on a solid footing that can weather the storms of corporate change. Not only can a good plan make your dreams more realistic if you have doubts, it also can serve as a safety net if you have no doubts but should.

You'll find out how in the next chapter.

CHAPTER 5
ALWAYS HAVE A PLAN B

CHOICES

BY BOMBARDING us with an onslaught of changes, life presents us with an endless succession of decisions. The way many people respond is to mistakenly view themselves as boxed in—with no good choices, some that are undesirable, and a great many that would bring them nothing but misery.

The way Bill Sergeant saw things, most of the alternatives he faced were so awful that he really had no choices at all. Bill and I recently had a long talk in the parking lot of a cemetery. We had just attended the funeral of a mutual friend when Bill suddenly opened up to me with details on what seemed like virtually every problem in his life.

Before I say what those problems are, you should know that Bill spent the first twenty years of his career in sales at a local car dealership, finally buying the place himself six or seven years ago, when the old owners retired. He put his house up as collateral, and everything else was leveraged on loans. By the time he and I had our little talk, the business was his and he was making a buck at it, but he was far from jumping for joy.

He complained about how nothing lasts anymore. The showroom at the dealership looked shabby and had to be refurbished at considerable expense. At the same time, state inspectors told him that the diagnostic equipment in the service bay was obsolete and did not meet the latest regulations.

Those were just his opening salvos. From the outrageous demands the union was allegedly making to the employees who he thought were cheating on their time cards to the suppliers who were overcharging him and to the competitors who were taking away his fleet accounts, I heard it all.

The more he talked, the more I felt compelled to ask a question: "Why don't you get out, Bill?"

"Whaddya mean?" he snapped.

"Sell the stupid business." I responded. "If it's causing that many headaches for you, it isn't worth it."

His reaction to my advice was amazing. With as straight a face as he could muster, he looked right at me and said, "I couldn't do that, Bob."

"Why not?" I asked.

"I have no choice," he answered. "I need the money that place brings in, my family needs it, and I want to leave it to my kids so they can leave it to their kids. Besides, most of my employees are good people who count on me to keep the place going; I can't abandon them."

That sounded reasonable, but I wasn't satisfied. "Then why don't you take off for a few days? You're not going to do anyone any good if you're too tired to think straight."

His answer sounded too much like the last one. "I'd love to get away, but there's really no one I can leave in charge, so I have *no choice* but to stay here and make sure things get done right."

Bill took the same approach to everything. He complained about how much it was going to cost him to pay for three hundred people at his daughter's wedding, so I suggested that he eliminate half the guest list, but he wouldn't hear of it. Once again, he had "no choice." This time his excuse was concern about offending this relative, that friend, or those important customers.

Poor Bill. He was a man without options, condemned to a life that he couldn't bear and yet had no way of escaping. Isn't that a shame? No. To my way of thinking, it was more of a sham, and that's what I told him.

"*Fred* has no choices," I said to Bill as I pointed over toward the grave where we had just been standing. "You have plenty of choices."

I don't mean to minimize Bill's problems. He may have blown some of them out of proportion, but they were real. They were also significant, but they weren't unsolvable. Of course he had choices. That morning when we met, for example, he chose to take what he felt was the only step he could take without penalty, which was to let off steam by talking to me, and then to continue doing what he had been doing or not doing all along.

You may not have Bill's wherewithal, and you might just love to trade places with him and suffer through all his "problems," but I'll bet that the two of you have a lot in common. Bill didn't have many problems, he had only *two* of them: great difficulty in acclimating himself to the surprises associated with change, and an absence of planning to deal with those surprises. These are the same two problems most people have with regard to change. Whether you can handle those problems is *not* a function of how much money you have but rather of how ready you are for the unexpected.

This is not that hard. You don't have to enjoy the difficulties associated with change. All you have to do is accept them as inevitable facts of life, and prepare yourself for whatever they are most likely to be.

FROM HERE TO THERE

Do you want your career to be somewhere other than where it is right now? All you have to do is identify your goal, point yourself in the right direction, and go until you get there. You can look it up in Chapter 4.

But hold on a minute. What would you do if the fastest way

to go in the right direction meant jumping off a cliff? If you had half a brain, you'd find an alternate way to reach your goal as fast as possible, a way that would not require you to risk your life or defy the laws of gravity. My guess is that you have *more* than half a brain. How much more may be arguable, but surely you realize that as important as goals are, they aren't enough.

A goal, you see, does only one job; it defines what you want as a result, the end point of a journey. If where you are now is here, your goal can be thought of as there. Starting here, you can get there only after providing yourself with intelligent answers to several questions:

- What's the best route to take?
- Partway there, how can I tell if I'm on track?
- How long is the trip?
- Who can help do what? What inducements can I provide in return?
- What supplies (resources such as specific skills or cash up front) will I need to get started? Which should I take with me? Which can I gather along the way? How and when can I best get the rest?
- What if I get lost? How can I find my way back?

Taken together, the answers to these questions are the underpinnings for your plan. If you have no plan, you are reduced to dealing with things as they arise, developing strategies off the top of your head, and winging it as you take care of problems on the fly. This may be challenging, exhilarating, and quite necessary when unforeseen emergencies arise, but it's a poor substitute for planning.

Only if you have a plan will you have at your fingertips the answer to a crucial question: *To meet my goals, how much of what kinds of effort should be applied by whom at which locations, at which times, and under which circumstances?* The best you may be able to do is guess, but if you don't have a reasonable facsimile of an answer, you don't have a plan. That's bad, because a goal without a plan is an end without a means, a punch line without a joke, or a great place to go without a way of getting there.

THE STRUCTURE OF PLANNING

A basic plan consists of five elements:

1. **Desired end results**—your goals.
2. **Method of accomplishment**—techniques you will use to get those results.
3. **Who has to do what?**—What do you have to do to make the plan work? Will others be required to assist you? Who? What are their roles?
4. **Necessary resources**—the specific amount of money and other resources that will be required at which points in time.
5. **A schedule with milestones**—Milestones are points along the way that you can use to determine whether you are going in the right direction or ahead of or behind any timetable you select.

Others have written in great detail about how to implement a plan, so I will not bore you with information that has appeared elsewhere. I am listing these elements for two reasons, the first of which is to save you the trouble of looking them up. My second reason is more complex, because only by showing you what a basic plan includes can I make clear what it does *not* include: allowances for change.

This is not to say that plans are worthless in helping you recognize the presence of change. To the contrary, a good set of milestones will be invaluable in helping you distinguish between what you are doing and what you should be doing to reach your goals when you'd like to reach them. They will also let you know if you are on the right track at any point in time, or someplace else, way off course.

If something has happened, however, what the basic plan will *not* do is help you get back to where you want to be, doing what you should be doing. For that, your plan needs a sixth element:

6. **Contingency scenarios**—how you are going to adjust your tactics, timetables, or goals if you implement your plan and nothing happens or you move away from your goal instead of toward it.

If you can think of the first five steps of planning as plan A, you will see why step 6 is known as plan B: the backup plan for determining what you are going to do next if what you do first doesn't work. A basic plan unto itself, each plan B is structured of the same five steps as a plan A, the difference being that one is based on how you'd prefer things to happen, the other for being sure that you have choices in the face of change. If push ever does come to shove, as the saying goes, plan B may be the only part of your plan that matters.

When changes occur as a result of circumstances brought about by others, all you can do is react. If you do not have a response ready to put into effect on a moment's notice, however, you can't do anything until you have evaluated the situation, considered your alternatives, decided what to do, and started doing it. Does the universe stand still while you're going through all that? Do the people who cause change wait for you to respond before they come up with even more changes? And even if they did, can you think straight if you are rushed into making instant decisions?

You know the answers. More often than not, rushed thinking comes from gut feelings, not clear logic. To make things worse, when people are out to get the upper hand by hurling changes at you, they're not going to stop and wait until you are ready for them. Unless you act quickly and correctly, you'll be playing catch-up from the minute you start. By the time you get close to them, they'll be shoving new roadblocks in your path.

But suppose you weren't caught off guard. Let's say you realize that *birds* wing it, not people. So instead of deciding what to do on the spur of the moment, and rather than putting everything on hold until you can figure out how to proceed, you prepare a carefully thought out strategy, all ready to kick into high gear if changes start hitting close to home. That strategy is a contingency plan.

You do this kind of planning all the time, but you probably don't think of it as a big deal. Before you go on a business trip, for example, you probably get a cash advance. That's a plan. Is it a good plan? That depends on the size of the advance.

Suppose you have enough to pay for expenses and then you meet an important customer you'd like to take to dinner. What if some emergency comes up and you have to extend your trip a couple of days? Did you take enough money to take care of these extras? And how about extra clothes? Did you bring any? Being ready for these questions often makes the difference between success and failure on a routine business trip. That's why standard issue for many business travelers includes an extra change of clothes, bank cards for teller machines, and credit cards. Yet what do most people have to back ourselves up en route to their career goals? Nothing.

Put It in Writing

The smart move is to put your plans in writing. Written plans save you the agony of memorizing a lot of details. Not only that, committing your plans to paper is a plan B unto itself because it will avoid having to make your plans anew should you forget them.

But don't just write it all down and then stick it in a drawer. Nail it up on a wall. If your office is too public, find a place at home where you can see it every day as a constant reminder of where you should be as opposed to where you are as you pass from milestone to milestone.

Use whatever format you like for putting your plans in writing. Format isn't important. What's important is that your plan is measurable so you can track your progress against it as you go along, that it consists of all six elements I've described, and that it is realistic.

Make It Measurable

We've already talked in Chapter 4 about the need to make your goals highly specific. The same applies to your methods of reaching them. Being smarter than the next person, Giving a 110 percent, and other such slogans are useless—unless of course you work in the poster, sign, or bumper-sticker business.

To the greatest extent possible, set your goals so they can be stated in the form of measurable milestones. Good examples are getting a certain promotion, reaching a designated salary level, working on a particular product, or being assigned to a specific job in a specific department.

Some goals are not easy to gauge until you attach milestones to it. A good example is wanting to become an expert in some subject. Will you have met your objective by taking and passing courses? Earning academic degrees? Understanding phenomena? Memorizing lists? Impressing people? Authoring books or articles on the related topics? Any or all of these criteria are okay, but *which* courses, degrees, phenomena, lists, people, and topics? *How many* books or articles? Answer these questions, tie each of them to a timetable, and you have yourself some milestones.

Time is a great yardstick. You can make any goal specific and measurable if you can tie it to a schedule. Not one with milestones every thirty seconds—that's not realistic. Pick the most difficult schedule you can live with—fast enough to get the job done, but not so fast that it needlessly rushes you. How fast is fast enough? That depends on how much of a penalty you have to pay if you delay your deadlines. If there is no delay and you can use the time productively on some other matter, do it. That's what it means to put your priorities to good use, and that's what time management is all about.

Keep It Realistic

A plan is realistic only if it meets four criteria:

- You are comfortable with it.
- It is doable without divine intervention.
- Given your circumstances and your resources, it takes you on the most direct route from here to there.
- In case it doesn't work, it is accompanied by a good backup plan to bail you out.

When you make a plan, you should think of it not as a straightjacket but as something to be referenced and updated as conditions dictate. Even if nothing changes except your projection of what's going to happen in the future, your plans will have to be fine-tuned or overhauled on a regular basis. To expect otherwise is unrealistic.

As bad as it is to have no plans, however, going overboard in the other direction is no better. If you try to be prepared for every conceivable contingency, you'll never get anywhere; everything you attempt will be prohibitively costly and take forever to get started.

To avoid getting stuck in a quagmire of excessive plans, determine which changes have the greatest probability of happening. Of those, eliminate anything you believe will cause only minor problems that you can easily deal with if they arise. What's left are the what-ifs, for which you should have a plan B.

In this regard, be careful of trying to choreograph your every move. You can rehearse the gist of what to say to your boss this afternoon or to a customer next week, but a plan cannot be a script. It can be only a guide that will help you think of that conversation or presentation as specific milestones to be reached on your way to a greater goal further down the road. Accordingly, long-range plans are most meaningful if they are light on the details while heavy on big-picture directions for meeting overall goals.

Short-range plans are quite another story. They are most

meaningful if they are designed so that each milestone is a mini-goal unto itself, the achievement of which requires a mini-plan.

Baskets

Tim Baker didn't care about contingencies early in his career. He had a goal—a good one. He wanted to be chief engineer in a field I used to work in: engineering acoustics. He also had a plan, in which his method of accomplishment was to impress his employer by doing as good a job as is humanly possible and to let his good work speak for itself.

After a few years, Tim was right on target; he was a nationally recognized expert in aircraft noise control, and he had "paid his dues" by working his way up through the ranks. And work he did—often sixty or more hours a week, with an occasional weekend, too. The extra time didn't bring him any extra money, but he figured it would pay off in the long run.

What Tim did *not* have was a plan B to see him through in case anything went wrong. This lack of forethought nearly destroyed his career when the aerospace industry became unglued during a recession some years ago. As business slowed down, companies started cutting back, jobs were eliminated, people were being laid off by the busload, and those employees who weren't let go began jumping ship in ever-increasing numbers in favor of more stable places of employment.

Tim was too busy concerning himself with his employer's welfare to think of his own best interests. Convinced that he could always find a good job elsewhere with his credentials, he refused to rush into changes he might regret. By the time he realized what was happening, most of the good slots in other businesses were already snapped up by those of his coworkers who were more awake to the facts of business life.

So no matter how bad things looked, he never quit, and neither was he fired. He stayed until the place went under, with his last assignment being to inventory the furniture for the supply house that bought it at auction.

He got another job, but it took him fifteen months. Of course he had experience and credentials, but nobody had openings. Not knowing what else to do, Tim did what many people do in a crisis: He felt sorry for himself, he complained a lot, and blamed his problems on incompetent former bosses, shortsighted prospective bosses, or any other convenient target. No matter how hard he tried to apply them, none of these tactics worked. When he finally did connect, the new employer was out of state, the pay was nothing special, and relocating was almost as traumatic as losing his job.

Poor Tim. He had apparently forgotten a famous quote from Cervantes's *Don Quixote de la Mancha*. The original form of the statement I'm talking about was something to the effect that a wise man does not put all his eggs in one basket.

Cervantes died nearly four hundred years ago, but his words haven't lost any of their significance. Virtually every twentieth-century person on someone else's payroll puts his or her eggs in that one basket called a job. Take the job away or alter it dramatically, and what's left for most people is a big void, a series of personal and professional crises, or both.

In Tim's case, not only did he have just one plan, he had one source of income, one way to achieve creative expression, one means of providing for long-term security, one place to meet new friends, and one mechanism for using, sharpening, and displaying his skills. These were all one and the same: his job. When he lost that, he lost more than just his paycheck; he lost everything.

MINIMIZING YOUR VULNERABILITY TO CHANGE

The less you depend on a job, the less you stand to lose if it is taken from you or significantly altered in a manner not to your liking. If you didn't rely solely on plan A, you wouldn't have to rely solely on your job as the mechanism for meeting your career goals.

The word is *goals*, not *goal*. As I pointed out in Chapter 4, none of us has just one career goal. Each of us has different goals relative to different aspects of what we want out of our jobs and our lives. These include:

- monetary rewards
- the ability to do a specific type of work
- enjoyment
- creative fulfillment
- security
- opportunity
- social interactions with your intellectual and professional peers

How many of these are important to you? For each one that is, you need a separate plan A *and* a plan B to go with it. Here are some of the possibilities at your disposal:

- **Don't wait until you lose one job before looking for another.** You should always be on the lookout for new and better jobs. This is simple enough, but most people never do it. Force yourself. Every day, take a few minutes to study the help-wanted ads.

Aside from making sure that you don't needlessly get surprised by the forces of change, continuously looking for jobs also keeps you abreast of current salaries in your field so you won't be misled by management into thinking that your substandard wages are competitive. No matter how good your job is, there are others just as good and still others that are better.

You don't have to apply for other jobs if they are not good, but maybe you'll see something you *want to* apply for. Even then, you don't have to interview, and even if you do, you don't have to accept if an offer is extended. If you want to keep ahead of change, however, you do have to keep looking at all times to see what jobs are open, and you can't do that by reading the comics.

I know a woman who signed on as customer-service

manager for a local company. Her previous employer had shut down some months earlier, so she was happy to take the new job even though it was for about 20 percent less money than she had been making.

But she didn't want to give up the 20 percent, so she kept looking and a month later found something else for 10 percent *more* than what she originally wanted. She jumped at it, but on resigning the old job, she was stunned to discover that even though she had been there only a few weeks, she had made an excellent impression. The company matched the offer and she stayed. Lucky? No. Sharp? Yes. And motivated, too.

• **Find ways to be fulfilled away from work.** Many of us labor under the misconception that the light at the end of our career tunnel is retirement, when we can take it easy and do absolutely nothing. But we don't wait until our golden years for that. Pressured by our work, we think we should relax and unwind by spending our evenings and weekends lounging around, watching the boob tube, and stressing ourselves as little as we can.

This approach to life would be great if you were a carrot or a fig, but you're not. You can't fool me; you're a person and you actually *can* think with that head of yours. Human beings need intellectual stimulation at all times, not just during working hours. No matter how hard you try, you can't be happy acting like a turnip. You can be happy only if you act like a person.

What's the biggest difference between a person and a turnip? In your case, I can't be sure. For most people, the difference is that a person has a brain and a turnip does not. There is, however, a strong similarity; if it sits long enough without doing anything, a turnip will begin to rot, and so will a brain. Just like our muscles have to be used, flexed, and kept in shape to work at peak efficiency, our brains can easily become erratic and unreliable if they are allowed to get out of shape through lack of challenging work-outs on a regular basis.

I wish this were just a question of being able to think sharply at all times. It's actually much more than that. A turnip will not be at all upset about decaying, while the person in whose skull a brain resides has a high likelihood of becoming bored, unfulfilled, and unhappy if that brain does not have a steady diet of stimulation and challenge.

People are not turnips. Regardless of their age, if human beings are no longer intellectually energized on a regular basis, they may begin to lose their vitality and act as if they have forgotten how to think clearly.

This is in some cases why bright, energetic people who happen to be in their sixties suddenly become tentative and old—only because they instantly change from productive workers to retirees. Aging brings on certain physical and psychological problems that have nothing to do with how we choose to behave, but I'm not talking about those. I'm talking about the fact that you cannot get the most out of life at any age on a diet of nothing but a job that doesn't challenge you to think, weekends at the beach, card parties, and taking out the garbage.

Don't wait until you retire to find out how much you need to keep your mind stimulated. If you like your job, there's a reason why, and chances are it's not just the money. Maybe it's because you are allowed to work without someone breathing down your neck, maybe it's because you like interacting with people as you do, or maybe it has to do with the freedom to be creative in specific ways.

Whatever it is, if you are doing what you want to do at work, you will be stimulated and fulfilled. Both are prerequisites of any career goal. Without them, no matter how much money you're making, you won't enjoy your job. You'll get disenchanted, you won't be able to maintain any enthusiasm for what you're doing, and you'll be a sitting duck for changes forced on you by management and by others who want the same things you want.

But what would you do if you lost your job or if it was changed so radically that you hated it? What would you have left in your life—washing the dishes and paying the bills? Those are important, but they represent what you have to do, not what you want to do.

That's the beauty of having a plan B. You don't have to rely on a job for fulfillment. Every one of us has a different mix of skills that we are good at *and* that fulfill our needs to do and to create. To identify them, go back to the same process we discussed in chapter 4 about identifying career goals. Start by looking at what you do on the job. Break your work down by tasks. Do you write well? Type? Draw pictures? Take pictures with a camera? Fix or build things? How about skills that have nothing to do with your job? Maybe you can grow flowers, teach, design jewelry, translate, make pottery, program computers, or put calligraphy on invitations.

Make it a point to devote a significant portion of your free time to an activity you find interesting and satisfying. It can be similar to what you do at work, or something of a completely different nature. Joining an organization or two may help, and volunteer work might also fill the bill. Even if you provide your time and your services without charge, the enjoyment you get in return could be priceless as a backup that keeps you off rock bottom the next time change comes roaring into town.

• **Develop a backup source of income.** Some financial planners advise their clients to weather tough times by maintaining the equivalent of six months' income in a savings account or a safe, high-yield investment. What knuckleheads! Your only source of income is your salary, you have barely enough money to meet your needs this afternoon, and they talk as if you have six months' worth of spare change lying around for a rainy day.

I hope you know better than to even listen to people who are that far removed from reality. By all means save what you can, but keep in mind that what you can put away is probably not going to be enough. Think beyond salary, investments, and savings accounts. Can you mortgage your house? Sell jewelry or other possessions? How about a part-time job? Two part-time jobs instead of one full-time job? If you're in sales and business is slow, for example, you may be able to find a second job that fills in the gaps between commission checks. You wouldn't be the first.

Don't limit yourself by thinking that a second job has to be worked *after* normal working hours. A guy I once worked with raised an extra five thousand dollars one year just by getting up every morning at 4 A.M. to deliver newspapers *before* he went to work. A schedule like that can be brutal, but nobody's going to give you anything free of charge, so unless you were smart enough to marry into money,* you're probably going to have to work for it.

Still another backup is a business you can run from your home evenings and on weekends. Do some research at your local library or bookstore. You can get books and magazines devoted entirely to businesses you can get into for no more than a few hundred dollars.

Perhaps you can emulate my neighbor, who started out as a carpenter's assistant. His income was sporadic, but he didn't know what else to do until a job came up where a homeowner wanted an extra closet built into her bedroom. Intrigued, he began looking for people who would pay him to build new closets and organize existing closets with multiple layers of rods, extra shelves, and the like. He did the same with basements and garages. Not only did that part-time enterprise stabilize his income, it grew over the years into a thriving full-time business. Now he's the one with the assistants.

Whether you decide to build an investment portfolio or a small business, don't wait until you need it. One of the biggest problems when you're out of work is that if you spend

*That's okay. I wasn't, either, and neither was my wife.

all your time looking for a good job, you won't be able to spend enough time making money for your immediate needs. Worrying too much about today, on the other hand, may prevent you from having enough time to make sure that tomorrow will be better suited to your long-range interests.

This is why you must get your backup income source in motion long before trouble strikes. You'll be much more willing to take the prudent risks that are always necessary to achieve gains, your need to make sacrifices will be minimized, and, if your plans are good enough, you may not have to sacrifice anything.

• **Don't socialize exclusively with your coworkers.** Funny thing about friends you meet on the job; they have a way of remaining friends only as long as you work together. If you move into different companies or different departments of the same company, chances are you'll drift apart. You and your friends may have the best of intentions, but if you both rely heavily on your job as a source of friendships, you'll tend to be close to people you work with *now*, not those you formerly worked with.

Of course you can develop friendships with the people you work with. Just make sure that you have other friends as well. The more you depend on fellow employees as your only source of social interaction, the more you will talk about your job during the off-hours, the more you'll rely on the job as the focus of your life, and the deeper in the hole you'll be if that job gets snatched out from under you.

SKINNING CATS

There may be a million ways to skin a cat, but I'm sure they're all disgusting, so let's limit our discussion to contingency plans. There are only two ways to use them in dealing with change:

• As discussed in the previous section, one way is to minimize dependence on your job by figuring out what needs it meets and looking elsewhere to meet those needs.

• The second way is to stand your ground—not by abandoning your plan or leaving your job, but by being ready for surprises, by confronting change head-on as soon as it strikes, by working around it, and by taking advantage of it as best you can. Here are four examples:

The Sale Falls Through

This is the big one; when you close this order, you'll be the hero of the decade in the eyes of all the top bosses. Every day you get closer and closer to getting the customer to sign. And then just when you least expect any snags, the rug is yanked out from under you for reasons you never could have anticipated. The business of the customer you've been going after undergoes a major restructuring and the sale is put on hold for at least a year and maybe longer. More importantly, your goal is put on hold.

Is it? That's up to you. Was that the only prospective customer you can go after? The only product or service you can sell? If no one else could use whatever it is, you've got to go out and find yourself some new baskets for those eggs of yours. There *are* others, aren't there? Why haven't you been pursuing them all along? You can also maintain contact with the people who reorganized you out of a sale, but you don't have to depend on them.

A mistake made by many salespeople is to focus on only the big prospects. Wiser heads realize that ten dimes are worth the same as a silver dollar. Lose one dime of ten, and you still have 90 percent of your fortune. Lose one coin the other way, and you're left with a whole lot of nothing.

The Project You're Working on Gets Canceled

You've been having the time of your life designing an exciting new product. You go to your boss's office to report that not only is that product ready, it'll be the greatest thing since sliced bread. But he cuts you off before you can start, saying that the board of directors has just throttled back on expenses and that plans to introduce your new wonder have been put on the corporate back burner. Urging you to hang in until times are better, he suggests that you take the news as a business decision, not as a personal rebuke.

Take, shmake. You have at least six better choices:

1. Find out what frightened off the board. Perhaps you can come up with a way around their concerns.

2. If your employer won't come out with the product, perhaps they'd be willing to sell it to someone else at the right price. Perhaps you could convince the buyer to hire you to spearhead the new line.

   How would a competitor find out about the product? How would he find out about you? You'd tell him—with your boss's permission. If funds are that scarce, he might welcome your initiative. Then, you'd give prospective buyers enough to tweak their interest but not so much that they could do anything without you. Backing that up, you might even get their written assurances that you're part of the package and that it's going to cost them dearly if they make a deal and then drop you.

3. A company you approach may not be interested in buying the rights from your employer but may be interested nonetheless in hiring you to develop a competing product.

4. Your employer may not want to give you permission to speak to other companies, but depending

on what you say, how you say it, and whether you
have signed secrecy agreements, you may not need
that permission. Check with a lawyer.*

5. Ask your boss how much the company would want
for the product rights and try to secure financial
backing yourself.

6. Get a different job with a different company, perhaps in a different field, and, hopefully, less likely
to let you pour your blood, guts, and time into
something and then can it.

You Get a New Boss

For the first time in your career, you had a boss you could work
with. Evenhanded and fair, he didn't get in your way. Instead,
he always helped you get what you wanted as long as you helped
him get what he wanted. Notice I'm talking in the past tense,
because that boss has been replaced. Why? That's his problem.
Your problem is that what you were doing to impress the old boss
may not work on the new boss.

Your plan B in this case could start with your moving on to
another job, but it doesn't have to be that way. It could start with
observing the new boss and figuring out what you'll have to do to
impress him or her, and doing it, at least long enough to give it
a fair shake. For all you know, the new boss will be better than
the old one was. You can get out if things don't pan out, but for
that you'll need to back up your backup.

Plan C? Why not? The alphabet won't mind. If there's the
slightest chance that you'll need it, have it ready. The worst
that can happen is the best that can happen: You won't have to
use it.

---

*If you feel ethically bound to not reveal proprietary secrets, go with your gut and do
only what you feel you can live with. Just remember that no one but you has exclusive
access to your know-how in perpetuity. If your employer will in fact not use your ideas,
you may be well within your rights to take them elsewhere.

Who's Left After Management Bails Out?

There isn't much else that can go wrong where you work. First, the company's biggest customer defected to the competition and then your boss and his boss resigned to form yet another competitor. In response, management has initiated a brilliant series of bold moves—laying off a third of the people in manufacturing, consolidating four territories into two so they can get rid of half the sales force, and wiping out the advertising budget for the next six months.

These strokes of genius save money, but they leave the company virtually paralyzed, unable to sustain any growth, and incapable of effectively handling existing business. More and more customers jump ship, while more and more employees defect to safer havens.

So many have left that a big promotion is offered to you—no increase in money, but a lot more responsibility. Under normal conditions, you might have waited years before you would have moved into that high a job, but now no one else is left and the bosses don't have the big money to attract outsiders. At the same time, however, you are told that the corporation is actively looking for a friendly buyout by someone with enough money to turn things around.

This is the kind of situation you should be in more often. Management may be running out of options, but you aren't. You can:

- take the promotion and make something of it
- refuse the promotion but stay
- get away as quickly as you can. Among other possibilities, maybe your old boss could use you at his new company

What should you do? First, play What's the Penalty? as described on page 98. You'll probably see that your best bet is to accept the promotion *and* at the same time look for anything else you can find. This again puts you in a plan B, plan C mode, but so what?

Under normal circumstances, you'd be stupid to take on a bigger job without a corresponding increase in compensation. In this case, however, you have nothing to lose by taking management's offer, buying yourself some time, and seeing what you can make of it. If a buyer is found and you do well, you could be in on the ground floor of an excellent growth opportunity. If not, you are probably better off anyway, since you can now look for new employment under the auspices of moving on from a higher level job than you had to begin with.

As long as you back yourself up by aggressively looking for a better opportunity elsewhere, refusing the promotion would be pointless. You can always tell them tomorrow that you have changed your mind and accepted another job.

TRAITS IN COMMON

My purpose in describing specific situations has been to show you how contingency planning is done, not to give an example of every possible use of a plan B. Circumstances and goals vary from person to person and situation to situation, so be careful in modeling your plan after what someone else has done. I suggest that you instead play What's the Penalty? in considering your options, and keep in mind the five traits that are typically present in a good plan B:

1. It is realistic and based on reason, not fear or any other gut feeling.
2. You can readily tell how it is doing compared to expectations.
3. It can be implemented at your discretion as soon as your plan A shows itself incapable of meeting your final goal or even a milestone.
4. To whatever degree is practical, it has its own es-

cape hatch in terms of a plan C and maybe even
a plan D.

5. Its success is predicated on your taking decisive
action. A plan will not work by itself; it will work
only if you make it work.

No choices? I don't believe it. If this, that, and everything
else is forever catching you by surprise and forcing you to stop
and then start all over again, your problem isn't change or a lack
of choices, it's a lack of contingency planning. No, you'll never
be able to foresee all future needs, and yes, thinking on your feet
will always be valuable. If you want to stop playing catch-up all
the time, however, wise up. To pull ahead and stay ahead, your
best bet is to plan ahead.

Your choices may be difficult and painful, but they do exist—and if you have a plan B, you'll know what they are. Until
you are lowered into the ground in a pine box, you will *always*
have choices.

CHAPTER 6
THE SHORTEST ROUTE TO JOB SECURITY

POLITICS

LET'S SAY that . . .

• Your boss just got fired. This is good, because in spite of
all your wishful thinking, you really didn't want a piano to fall
on the little weasel, you just wanted him out of your life. Instead
of being happy, however, you're enraged—not because of second
thoughts about the piano, but because you didn't get a promotion
out of the deal.

Someone else got that plum; someone you haven't even met
yet: a carpetbagger who was hired in from another company. The
only thing you got was a memo from that person asking for a
summary next week on the work you've been doing.

You're so ripped at being bypassed that you'd just as well
hand in your resignation, but nobody died and left you a fortune,
so you can't afford rash actions. Can you still come out a winner
here? How?

• You've just received the announcement of the company picnic, and you don't have to read between the lines to see that attendance is pretty much mandatory. This annual event was bad enough under the old management, but they've been bought out and an afternoon with the new owner is abominable, even worse if you are downwind of him.

You could say your brother had an accident and you had to visit him in the hospital, but somebody might catch on; you used that excuse last year and you don't even have a brother. Do you have to go to that picnic? If so, how can you profit from being there?

• If your salary isn't increased in the near future, you're going to be in trouble. Hell, you *are* in trouble, deep trouble; you're dead broke. Sales being way off, however, raises are hard to come by these days. And as if that weren't bad enough, you do not get along with your boss. The way the two of you have been sparring lately, you couldn't convince her to give you the time of day, much less a raise. You've tried to get another job, but nothing is out there. What can you do until something comes along?

You know I'm going to say that you have choices in each of these situations, but you'll better appreciate what those choices are if we hold off discussing them until later. First, can you see what these anecdotes share? What they share is that none of them can be dealt with by a knowledge of economic cycles, companies, papers of incorporation, financial statements, or productivity. They can be dealt with only by the judicious application of "people" skills.

Take a look around. Who are the winners and the losers where you work? Many a boss with average intelligence and mediocre job talents has fought his or her way to success fueled only by sheer drive combined with a masterful expertise at manipulating everyone in sight.

At the same time, a far greater number of brilliant, highly capable individuals are unhappy and unsatisfied. Unable to reach their goals, they are losers. This is not because they lack talent. Some of them have a lot of talent, but they don't understand that in most instances, the only way to manage change on the job is to become an expert at the much-maligned yet often misunderstood art of office politics.

VALUE ADDED

A common perception of success is that the only way to get ahead on the job is to think only of yourself and to do what you want to do, without the slightest concern for how others may be affected by your actions. Equally common is the idea that the best way to attain job security is to swallow your pride and cave in to every demand your boss makes of you.

Neither of these images is true. Indicative of behavior that rarely provides maximum satisfaction, both are gross oversimplifications. The trick to surviving in a changing world is realizing that putting yourself first does *not* mean putting anyone else last. As I'm about to show you, it usually means quite the opposite.

Some bosses are selective. They are well aware of how hard to push which people, when to back off, when to be affable, and when to reward their minions for a job well done. I think they are the best bosses, but they are not the only bosses. Others spew out a constant stream of expressed or implied threats designed to cause the work force to think that any lack of obedience will result in an unpleasant if not insecure future.

Such threats are not always carried out, but many employees make the mistake of presuming that the only way they can respond is to engage in what is known as sucking up to their bosses. A desire to keep this discussion out of the gutter keeps me from speculating on the origin of that term, but I can define it. It means being so afraid of bosses that you do things you don't want to do—just to keep them from getting mad at you. Taken to extremes, it means unhesitatingly obeying their every whim, no matter how demeaning, stupid, or counterproductive you find it, and regardless of how much it gets in the way of your personal plans.

Even on a moderate level such as making coffee for the boss,

sucking up is not only offensive, it doesn't work. It will *not* motivate people to think that you are an asset who cannot be replaced.
Unless you get a promotion because you are so incompetent that
you don't threaten anyone, it won't even help you get a better
job. It also puts you in a poor position from which to advance
toward your goals; motion is slow and painful if you never get up
off your knees.

Perhaps the worst part of sucking up, however, is that it all
too often puts you at the mercy of greedy egomaniacs who typically have no mercy. The more you do, the more they'll want and
the less they will give you in return.

What can you do? One school of thought is to fight fire with
fire, taking everything they throw at you and dishing out at least
as much in return. Rough-and-tumble battles of will are a way of
life for many people who have to survive from day to day under
difficult bosses.

The danger in that route is the ease with which it can fool
you into getting detoured. Launching an attack against a boss or
seeking revenge for his transgressions can easily divert your focus
from meeting career objectives to accumulating points in a bizarre
contest to see which of you wins each day's jousting. You can pile
up zillions of points, but if you do it in a way that embarrasses the
boss or forces him into a position he doesn't like, your name may
move right to the top of the list of those slated to go during the
next cutback.

A safer, more effective alternative is to observe your bosses,
to figure out their likes and dislikes, and to give them what *they*
want without sacrificing what *you* want. Companies do basically
the same thing when they lower their price to convince us that
their products have a high value. It's a sound business practice—as long as they don't drop prices so far that they can't get
the profits they seek. It's also sound on a person-to-person basis
as long as you don't give more than you get.

Before you dismiss this as nonsense, consider the way in
which the most powerful person in the world gets into office. One
does not become president of the United States by force; you can't
blast your way into the White House. You get there by convincing

others that they have more to gain by helping you than by fighting you.

It's so simple, it's beautiful. You join a group called a political party and you work for the good of its members. Give enough help to enough party members for a long enough time, and they'll return the favor. The more they do that, the more power you'll have—as a candidate for office, as a force behind the scenes within the party hierarchy, or as a political appointee.

Of course there's more to it than that, and of course there are generous helpings of competitive back stabbings of various kinds. The process works more often than not, however, because everyone owes favors to everyone else and because everyone is trying to make himself more and more valuable to everyone else.

The corporate world doesn't work in exactly the same way, but there are many similarities. Instead of political parties, companies have cliques, in-groups that are close to the seat of power. Another similarity—the most important of all—is that *the more valuable you become in the eyes of others, the more willing they will be to be valuable to you.*

The more valuable you are to your bosses, the more they will want to protect you, the harder they will fight to hold on to you, and the more willing they will be to give you special privileges. Make them look like fools or habitually get in their way, on the other hand, and you can be certain that they will view you with scorn. You would behave the same way if your roles were reversed.

There is no such thing as absolute job security with anything beginning to resemble ironclad guarantees. But if a secret exists for shielding yourself from the unwelcome effects of change, it is motivating the people in power where you work to believe that you are so valuable to their personal plans that dumping you or even getting you angry would be a mistake of humongous proportions.

Bosses will always make changes. You can't stop that. But if you persuade the right people to believe that you are more valuable than anyone except themselves, they will bend over backward to make certain that their changes don't hurt you.

MAKE PEOPLE FEEL COMFORTABLE WITH YOU

For people to think of you as being valuable, they must trust you at least enough to let you demonstrate your value. Before they will trust you, however, they must feel good about having you around. They should never see you as representing danger or even potential danger. Instead, your presence should make them feel safe and comfortable.

The traditional way to make yourself valuable is to work as hard as you can to produce as much as you can at the highest possible quality. You should never do anything less, but as I have already shown in Chapter 2, doing a great job doesn't help with some bosses. To the contrary, if they feel that their fears have been triggered or their egos bruised, they may respond to your efforts by creating changes you don't like.

Your challenge is to do a good job without making anyone uncomfortable with you. Here are more than a dozen ways to pull it off:

- **Make a good first impression.** At no time is the need for making a good impression on a person more important than the first time you meet that person. Many people are fearful and hesitant to believe or trust anyone. No matter how capable or how loyal we may be, they think of us as guilty of treachery, incompetence, or both—even before they have seen us in action. A bad first impression reinforces all that, but a good first impression can erase it.

In one of the scenarios posed at the start of this chapter, you were mad when the company hired someone from the outside instead of promoting you to the open slot created when your old boss got sacked. You haven't met this new boss yet, but he has sent you a memo asking for a summary of your work.

You can get angry at such a request, and you can give it as little attention as possible. You can even play for time by forgetting about it and claiming that you never got it in the first place. But you're too smart for such childishness, so you stop to think. You realize that the new boss has just been thrust into a stressful situation—a new job in a new company, with new colleagues, new subordinates, and new bosses. He may have had to give up seniority rights he had at his previous job, and he may have had to relocate. He has a lot invested in making this move and among the first things he's going to want to do will be to take command of his troops.

The last thing he'll want is an envious and uncooperative lieutenant whose knees are buckling under the weight of too many sour grapes. You have nothing to gain by creating that image for yourself. How *can* you gain? By making yourself so valuable that the new boss concludes that he'd be out of his mind not to capitalize on you. Is this the same as taking advantage of you? Not necessarily. Create the right impression, and the boss will want to take advantage not of you but of your presence as a valuable asset he can rely upon.

Welcome him. Say you're glad to see him on board, and offer to help out in any way you can. If he has had to move to take this job, you can also offer to show him around after hours and on weekends. With regard to that report summarizing your work, say that you're happy he asked for it and that you'll have it done on time.

Instead of looking at writing the report as an intrusion on your time, look at it as an opportunity. Don't just give cold facts and lists of activities that have been done and should be done; no lies, nothing implausible, and nothing that might be seen as fluffing up the truth, but just enough flavoring to make a good first impression and show how valuable you are.

What will this boss consider valuable—problems as he begins his new job? No. Decisions to make on subjects he isn't yet up to date on? Of course not. What he wants is to see that things are under control and that there aren't any disasters waiting to crash in on him. That's the tone your report should take: No surprises are anticipated, no difficulties are in sight that you can't handle, and everything is functioning according to a well thought out plan that you have already put into place. Go ahead and mention a few problems on the horizon, but point out how you have not only anticipated them but taken steps that will quickly solve them.

You are not going to write a report, you're going to write a masterpiece. What you are *not* going to do is be obvious. You'd come across as arrogant and make the new boss leery of you if you say that your performance has been brilliant, that your quick thinking saved the day, or that you are indispensable. So don't make any claims about your value. Present only the "right" facts, and the boss will come to the right conclusions all by his lonesome.

- *Example #1:* You're in sales and the most obstinate purchasing agent in your territory has finally retired. He was the best of friends with one of your competitors, but his replacement has an open mind and has given you some sizeable orders recently.

    What do you do—give the credit for the sales to the old goat's retirement? No way! Volunteer nothing about the retirement. Don't even say that the current buyer is new to the job. Say only that you have established an excellent rapport with the buyer at XYZ, who has recently come through with several large orders.

    This position establishes you as offering something of value in the form of a working relationship that can bring in business, but that value is to the company. To offer value to the boss himself, indicate that you look forward to introducing him to this buyer and all your other customers so you can help him establish his own good working relationships.

- *Example #2:* You came in under budget last year, and you didn't miss any deadlines. You feel this is due to your strong management style, but a little humility would sound better here. Just say, "All budgetary objectives met; no deadlines missed."

- *Example #3:* You believe that switching to a new design will reduce costs without compromising product integrity, but your former boss was too set in his ways to pursue your ideas. Now that he is gone, tell the new boss you'd like to meet with him to get his views on your plans for slashing expenses.

   Do *not* however, say what those plans are. Bait a hook, one that will draw the new boss toward wanting to meet with you to see what you have in mind.

   Don't bend the truth to suit your needs. If you do, reality may someday bite you where it hurts. Stay with the facts, but instead of dumping all of them on paper, choose them carefully and state them in such a way that in the absence of other information, the boss cannot help but form whatever first impression you want him to form.

As the coup de grace, precede the report with a cover letter that offers your assistance in helping the boss in any way you can, while saying that you invite his comments. Close by saying that you look forward to helping him set up long-range plans in the coming months. There's no need to fawn or gush. Just offer your help from one human being to another, one professional to another.

- **If you want the part, look the part.** One of the easiest ways to make a good first impression has nothing to do with being competent or valuable. All you have to do is take on the appearance and demeanor that will be seen as representative of a high-class professional.

   I didn't know about the importance of appearances when I was a kid. Things were simple then. You could go to the movies and see at a glance who were the good guys and who were the bad guys. It was easy: The good guys were well groomed and wore clean clothes—often white, to accentuate their supposed purity of purpose. Most of the bad guys, on the other hand, were dirty, wore black, and looked as if they hadn't shaved in days.

   Then I grew up. Or at least I got bigger, older, and wise enough to know that looks tell you nothing. Hitler was immaculately dressed. For more current examples, check out the garb of drug dealers when they are hauled before a judge. There they are, the scum of the earth, trying their hardest to look respectable in the eyes of a jury of their "peers." How? By wearing tweed suits and other finery that would get them laughed out of their usual habitats.

In the realm of so-called legitimate businesses, it's hard to tell the good guys from the bad guys or the geniuses from the jerks. Every last one of them wears suits. The people convicted of insider trading in recent years, for example, drape themselves in only the finest, cleanest, and latest clothes. Their hair is fashionably styled, they are spotless from head to toe, and they can be trusted as far as you can throw the stock exchange.

Okay, so business suits may not be the usual outfit in your field. Maybe it's swimsuits, or jeans and a T-shirt. Whatever it is, wear it. As much as you might want to stand out on the job, you can't do that unless you first blend in and make people feel comfortable with the way you look. Most people don't realize how meaningless appearances are. As long as you look good to them, their gut feel will be that you *are* good.

• **Smile.** No matter who you meet or work with, they will not find you valuable if you greet them with a facial expression of the sort one might use in reacting to the presence of an ax murderer.

If you don't concern yourself with the impression you make on others, that's precisely what may happen. Suppose you are deep in thought trying to solve some perplexing problem. Frustrated at not getting the right answers, you may look angry, upset, and ready for battle.

Anyone who walks up to you while this is going on might think you are frowning, that you are the bearer of bad news, or that you *are* bad news. If someone hasn't met you before and has a cynical bent, she may even write you off before you have a chance to show how valuable you are.

This is where a smile can come to your rescue. A real smile, not the phony variety. It costs nothing, consumes no more time or effort than a scowl, and yet even with a face like yours, it can work wonders. All it has to do is to look genuine. A smile is often the first part of a good first impression.

Flash your pearly whites at them, and people may be fool enough to think you are happy to see them or that you bring good news. At the least, they'll conclude that you do not bring bad news. I know it's simplistic to make yourself valuable by smiling, but I also know it works.

• **Remember the amenities.** Money, and profits are powerful motivators, but as words they don't begin to have the clout of "thank you" and "please." By using these expressions, you tell one and all that their efforts are valued and their cooperation is not taken for granted.

And don't forget to say hello to when you meet people. Ask how they are, but not in a perfunctory way and not in a way that lets them off the hook by responding with, "Fine" or something else of equal nothingness. If you can, get them to feel at ease by inquiring about their children, their new car, or anything else they might like to brag about.

• **Emphasize what you have in common.** One of the best ways to make people comfortable with you is to demonstrate that you have a lot in common with them. Typical examples are similar interests, opinions, and feelings on social and political issues, as well as the same enemies and dislikes.

Do you report to someone who is wary or even afraid of people who might look better than he does? Perhaps he would better appreciate your value if, without being obvious, you were to:

• suggest ways in which he would be able to interfere with the plans of people he considers to be his enemies.

• figure out who he thinks are his worst enemies and provide him with information and assistance for defeating or controlling those individuals accordingly. If he doesn't gossip or divulge his enemies list, make your own choice of who he probably hates the most, fears the most, or would most like to control. Who, for example, would be most likely to give him a hard time on that new project he's working on? Or with whom would he be most likely to compete for a promotion if his boss left, died, or got transferred?

• tell him any office scuttlebutt he may find interesting—not gossip or nonsense, but real meat he might be able to use to solidify his position or to conquer those he thinks of as his enemies.

• **Listen.** There are times when even the most hard-boiled among us wants to talk to someone—not to confide anything secretive or personal, but just to expound on whatever or whoever is on his mind. You can be extremely valuable to such a person simply by being attentive, while giving the impression that you agree (or at least don't disagree) with whatever point of view he is expressing.

After you have listened enough to figure out what another person's thinking is and after you are absolutely convinced that he or she is finished talking, latch on to something you can identify with and use it to show that you feel the same way. The next time you meet, try to find yet another area of like interest. The more you can come up with and take advantage of, the more you will be treated as a trusted, valued ally.

But never assume that people are interested in your problems. Quite the opposite may be true. They also may not want your advice, in which case any suggestions you volunteer might be misconstrued as presumptuous. The only exception is commiserating when someone is complaining about a problem similar to one you have had.

Tune in to anyone who will talk to you, not just bosses. You never know who may be able to help you someday, who may appreciate your taking the time to listen, or who may have some news of interest.

If you are asked for your advice and you are reasonably sure that it will work, give it. Providing input or opinions that people want is part of what increasing your value is all about. The more you talk, however, the less the person to whom you are listening can say. Listening is best performed with your ears, not with your mouth. People may not be comfortable with you if they have to assertively shut you up to squeeze in a few words now and then. Neither will they find you valuable if you force your opinions on them.

Never attempt to fake it when listening. Concentrate as hard as you can on what people say to you: not what you'd like them to say, not on what you want to say to them, and not what someone is saying in the next office. You can't do this while you are talking, doing something else, or thinking about something else. If you can't give people your undivided attention, meet them again at a time when you can.

Fail to listen carefully, and you run a great risk of slipping up, losing your train of thought, and showing that you weren't paying attention. Easily interpreted as a slap in the face to the person who is talking to you, this will diminish your value, not increase it.

Listening will give you an earful of more than problems: You'll hear what the other person likes and does not like. After someone becomes comfortable in opening up to you, other information may also be forthcoming, such as who is in his or her favor and why. Armed with this new knowledge about what that person considers valuable behavior, all you have to do is display it as much and as often as you can.

• **Let them think that you think they are important.** When people talk to you, don't just listen and soak in what they say, give them the impression that they and their boneheaded ideas are important. People whose thinking is ego-dominated will find nothing more valuable. Ask them to explain further. Pepper your conversation with an occasional, "That's fascinating!" or, "You don't say." Remember the amenities and thank them for taking the time to fill you in on their thoughts.

Go to them and solicit their advice. Don't wait for them to come to you, and don't admit or suggest that you can't proceed without their input; they may see that as a sign of weakness and attack or undermine you accordingly. Instead, be positive. Frame your request for help around a situation that is allegedly perplexing you, put forth the pros and cons of a decision you are making relative to that situation, and ask for assistance on specific aspects of that decision.

At the beginning of this chapter I asked how you might avoid going to the company picnic you hate so much. Have you come up with some devious ways out? Forget them all. If you have firmly established your value, you probably won't be fired just for boycotting the barbecue. You would, however, be shortsighted; the picnic offers you an excellent opportunity to increase your value to the boss by developing something in common with him. Unless you have other plans, a couple of hours on a Saturday afternoon is a small price to pay for that large a reward.

When you arrive, you'll see your peers hovering around the boss and telling him how great they think the picnic is. Even now, you can close your eyes and picture them scraping their lips off his rear end after they make sure he knows they are present and accounted for. Of course you make it known that you have arrived. Shake his hand and say hello with as genuine a smile as you can muster. But instead of talking about business or how happy you are to be there, come at him from a direction he won't expect and ask for his help on a personal matter.

If you do this right, the boss will eat it up; he'll be flattered to see that while everyone else is sucking up, you are seeking his advice on a matter outside the realm of work.

The problem is that it takes a level of guts and devilishness that many people just don't have. If you think you are up to it, however, make things easy on yourself and choose a subject that really is of interest to you. You won't have to put on much of an act that way, and you will be that much more convincing.

You could do this during the week, but by doing it at the picnic, you make a much better impression than your fellow employees; they are merely groveling, while you are telling him what he wants to hear. And you are not being obvious. How can you be sure he will want to grant your request for assistance? You can be sure by picking a subject that you know is important to him.

The possibilities are endless:

• His office wall features several pictures of him at his favorite outside activity. Tell him you would appreciate any recommendations he might have that would help you to buy a boat, some fishing gear, a set of golf clubs, or whatever else is appropriate to that activity.

• You could say that your son is interested in the same college his daughter is attending. Ask how she likes it and whether the school lives up to its reputation.

• Inquire about his car, briefcase, electronic notebook, or anything else he owns and enjoys. Claim that you are interested in a similar purchase and want his recommendations.

• Ask him to confirm his interest in photography, classical music, or some other hobby that you know commands his attention. Then solicit his suggestions on books or courses that would help you learn about that subject.

Take no more than a minute or so to plant the seeds of seeking out the boss's advice, and pose your questions in such a way that yes or no answers will not suffice. Ask if you can complete the discussion some night during the following week if he is available. He'll also want to hear that, since it means that neither of you will be distracted during normal working hours.

Do your homework, and be prepared. Don't try to substantiate a boss's interest in historical novels if he has just given a speech on one of them. Similarly, you should avoid discussing any subject unless you have studied it enough to carry a conversation to the point of demonstrating that your own interest is genuine. Before you plunge into a conversation about a certain car or camera, for example, look at it, listen to the sales pitch on it, read the manufacturer's brochures, and make some notes you can memorize. You'll ruin everything if you give the slightest hint that you are insincere or that your motives are anything other than what you have stated them to be.

• **Never be threatening or judgmental.** One way you can be unintentionally threatening is to be critical or judgmental when all someone wants of you is sympathy and compassion. You may think you know the advice that is in his or her best interests, but is that the advice which would be most appreciated? If it isn't, you had better think long and hard before you give it.

To get bosses and others on your side, you have to convince them that you are on their side, or at least not *against* their side. They must sense that you do not threaten them in even the slightest, most unintentional way. Show them no signs indicating that your goals are in conflict with theirs.

If your boss displays a fixation on being the hero in the eyes of top management or the rest of his people, let him be the hero. That way, you'll be far more valuable to him and far more secure than would be the case if you were to hog the glory. To illustrate this point, assume you are in a meeting with your boss and his boss, who says something that's a mistake. What should you do?

1. Point out where he goofed.
2. Slip him a note so he can correct himself before anyone notices.
3. Slip the note to your boss so *he* can pass it on.

You can select A and win the battle, but if his majesty's ego doesn't like to be corrected, that choice might force you to lose the war. You could also choose B. That could make you a hero in the big boss's eyes, a result that might not make your boss particularly happy. The best answer is C. That way, your boss can be a hero in his boss's eyes, you can be a hero in your boss's eyes, nobody loses, and everybody wins.

• **Don't box people into a corner from which they can't escape.** You and your boss are having a disagreement. He's wrong, *very* wrong. You have data and reports from a dozen outside experts as well as from customers, competitors, and government agencies. He usually gets the best of you, but now you've got him. There's no way he can win this argument.

Maybe not. But as long as he's the boss, he can lose and send you packing tomorrow. Instead of bludgeoning him with proof, give him the evidence and let him make up his own mind. If you know from previous discussions that agreeing with you would in effect force him to feel embarrassed, let him save face. Point out that the information you have just shown him was previously not available or that it was misinterpreted when it was first explained to him. You might even say that you were the one who did the misinterpreting. Another possibility is to discuss the matter with him in private, where he won't have to injure his ego in front of others.

No one likes to get boxed in, and we tend to have long memories about who did the boxing. Even if we did it ourselves, we may not want to take the blame, preferring instead to lay at least a part of the fault at someone else's feet.

Your bosses and the other people you work with are no different. They won't like you if they think you contributed to their losing an argument, making a wrong decision, or losing face. Sometimes, the best way to be valuable to your boss is to be the person who opens up doors that allow him to escape. You can:

- offer excuses ("we just got some new data you didn't have earlier") that let him explain his mistakes as being beyond his control and not due to his incompetence.
- identify scapegoats on whom he can blame his mistakes.
- if you can avoid hurting yourself in the process, jump in and say something, take action, or assume the scapegoat role yourself and divert pressure away from him.

• **Look 'em right between the eyes.** Don't look at your watch or out the window when someone is talking to you. Keep an unwavering focus on his or her eyeballs. Even if you aren't paying attention, you'll look as if you are thinking about nothing other than what that person is saying. Open up your own eyes as wide as possible. Someone who is bug-eyed looks astonished and perhaps silly to the casual observer, but not to the talker who seeks your ear and your concern. To that person, you will look involved and sincerely interested, which is exactly how you want to look.

• **Make life easy for the people who can make things easy for you.** Perhaps the person to whom you report wants to work in a certain way on certain projects, unencumbered by other responsibilities. If that's the case, volunteer to take on (or at least help out with) the other items on his agenda, and he may see you as the most valuable person in town. This goes double if you agree to do something he considers unpleasant, such as sitting in at those awful staff meetings his boss conducts or running out to buy a birthday present he can give his wife or his secretary.

• **Keep them informed.** You may be more valuable to a boss if he feels he always knows what you are up to. If that means updating him every hour or so, do it. This may be a waste of company time, but it certainly isn't a waste of your time, particularly if your bosses are in the grip of fear. The more they know about what you are doing, the less they will have to worry about the troubles you might bring on them.

• **Keep it up.** A good first impression is no place to stop. You may not be fortunate enough to be working with people who think of you as being valuable for what you did last week, or even yesterday. They may have short memories and be interested only in what you can do for them today.

Look at every impression as a first impression, with each being just as important as the other. No matter what you did in the past, take nothing and no one for granted; find something else you can do to be sure that the value you offer is always current.

If making people comfortable with you sounds something like a public-relations campaign, that's exactly what it is. Of course facts are important, but what you are is nowhere near as important as what the other guy *thinks* you are. The way people perceive the facts always carries more weight than the facts themselves. If you can control the way you are perceived by the right people, you'll be able to twist them right around your finger—whenever you like and to whatever extent you like. And I'm not talking only about bosses.

NETWORKING, CULTURE, AND CULTS

Okay, let's assume that your boss thinks you are valuable. That's terrific, but if the story ends there, you're not yet even close to being ready for change. As powerful as they may be, bosses don't hold all the aces.

To get to the people who do, you have to worm your way into the culture where you work. Culture? That's the net effect of an organization's traditions and pecking orders. Once you understand a company's culture, you'll know what makes that company go, what makes it stop, and who has to be motivated in which ways to get different results.

Any idiot can look at an organization chart, but managers hold only a part of an organization's power and hierarchy is only part of a company's culture. The other part is understanding how people use their power, how to reach them, and what kinds of incentives one has to offer to move their thinking in one direction or another.

At one corporation with which I am familiar, the president spends most of his time in the lab doing advanced research. That's what he likes, so that's what he does. He delegates everything else to others, keeping up to date by means of a weekly staff meeting.

He's not the only one whose job is not entirely indicative of his title. The chief engineer, for example, runs only a part of the engineering operation. He ran all of it years ago, but now he works almost full-time writing technical papers and representing the company in trade groups and civic associations. Why? Because he turned out to be too methodical to meet the fast-paced demands of the special projects that now make up the bulk of the company's business. Who handles those? The marketing manager, of course: He's a workaholic who happens to be good at design as well as sales. And if you think that's odd, the manager of the maintenance group doubles as the human-resources chief.

In another company, the owner keeps all formal power to himself. Five hundred employees work there, however, and as high an opinion as the boss might have of himself, he can't supervise them all, second-guess them all, or do all their work for them. That's why he assigns certain key jobs to key people who have gained his trust. You won't see their names on an organization chart, but that doesn't mean they lack power.

The two companies I have just described have more in common than you might think. Both seem to succeed in spite of the ways in which they are run, but the truth is that they succeed *because* of the way they are run. All organizations are like this in one way or another. Run on the basis of *cults* of personality, they dispense power not only from the person at the top but also from others to whom that person listens or delegates authority.

Find out who these others are where you work and what you have to do to make yourself valuable to them. They can react to you in any of three ways: They can be your ally; they can be your enemy; or they could not care about you one way or the other. You could react to them in like fashion, but you'd be a fool not to try to make as many friends as you can.

This has nothing to do with ethics, morality, or an altruistic interest in being a nice person. Neither does it have anything to do with turning the other cheek. It's a matter of mathematics. If your friends are more powerful than your enemies, you're going to be difficult to hurt. Make enough enemies, on the other hand, and they may eventually gang together and flatten you, no matter how good you are at your work. That's why the smart money is on you only if you have as few adversaries as possible while cultivating as many allies as you can find.

Think of yourself as planting the seeds for your future. Would you put just one seed in the ground? No—that would be the same as having no plan B. Sow as many seeds as you can; the acorns you cultivate today may not produce mighty oaks tomorrow, but given enough time and nurturing, they might eventually give you an entire forest. Examples are:

• *Accounting*. They'll know when the company where you work has cash-flow problems or difficulty paying its bills.

• *Sales*. They'll be able to tell you (or at least should know) about sales trends management may not want to publicize.

• *Shipping*. They'll know right away if anything is slowing down or speeding up.

• *Customers*. They may tell you what the competition is doing and what you might be able to do accordingly to make a hero of yourself. Gouging customers on price and making promises you can't meet will turn them into enemies who may

not even want to talk to you anymore, much less be valuable
to you.

In contrast , treating them fairly can pay off with more
business, with respect for you as a professional, and with advice in the right direction should you ever need their help.

• *Suppliers.* The people from whom you get goods and services are often an excellent pipeline to what's going on in your
industry or in other parts of your own company. Give them a
fair shake, and if you're in trouble they may at least give you
advice on who can assist you if they can't.

• *Competitors.* You may get job offers if they have openings, but only if they know of your good reputation.

All these people are integral parts of a network of contacts
you can have working for you. And they're just a part of what
a fully developed network can be. Think of the departments
with which you interface regularly. Who are the bosses there?
Can you make yourself valuable to them? They may have
nothing to offer you now, but they might come in handy someday. You can never tell when you can be the hero of the day
by cashing in on a favor owed to you by a manager in another
department. If not the managers, who can you reach on their
staffs? Figure out the answers, make a list, and get to all of
them, one at a time.

All of us have the same on-the-job needs: to grow in accordance with our ambitions and abilities, to be secure, to be intellectually satisfied, to be happy, and to be occasionally recognized
for our skills and good work. On top of all that, the people with
whom you work may or may not be obsessed with power and
riches, but you can bet they would enjoy a generous serving of
each once in a while, along with any edge they can get on their
competitors and their enemies.

You may not be able to distribute influence, give raises, or
hand out awards to anyone, but you may be able to help people
be satisfied or grow; you can probably help them be secure and
happy; you can definitely make their lives easier; and you can
often help them outfox their enemies.

Jan Cormack was a secretary at one of the fine establish-
ments where I used to work. She and I had the same boss, a
senior executive who used her as a tap into the company grapevine. Anything she overheard went right to him. It also went to
me and a small circle of other friends. She kept us up to date on
what she overheard in the executive suite. Jan was good, she was
discreet, and she knew who to trust.

Jan also controlled who got in to see her boss, which re-
quests for his signature got to the top of the pile, and who was
warned when he was in a lousy mood. She made sure I never had
any trouble accessing him, and she always kept me up to date
on who was in favor, who was in trouble, and who was on the
way out. What did I have to give her in return? When she got
snowed under, I made it my business to help out and to drag
along one or two others who owed me some favors. I also did my
own typing, so she didn't have to worry about getting my work
done.

Nate Freed and I had a similar arrangement. He had a lot
of personal problems: His wife was sick of him and he was sick
of his job, but he was also broke and they had a son who really
was sick. To take care of his son, Nate often had to come in late,
leave early, or vanish for an hour at midday. He'd put in extra
time to make up for any he missed, but our boss told us more
than once that death was the only valid excuse for being away
from work. So to whatever extent I could, without falling behind
in my own work, I covered for Nate. Big deal. I took his calls and
contacted a few customers on his behalf every once in a while. He
was good for it. When my own schedule needed some flexibility,
Nate was there when I needed him.

What do the people on your network need? Do you have
information they might want? A willingness to pitch in when they
have a problem requiring a couple of extra hands? Whatever it
is, find out what it is and give it or do it.

A good way to start increasing your value to someone in
your network is to make him look valuable to his boss. A
customer once called me to find out why our paperwork said
we were shipping a month *after* he wanted the products in his

plant. Looking into the situation, I discovered that we could ship on time but that the acknowledgment had the wrong date on it. All I could think of was to run over to see whether Alice, one of our production expediters, could help. I told her what happened, and the order was on the next plane out. The customer called the following day to thank me for getting him out of a jam.

That afternoon, I sent a memo to Alice's boss, thanking him for his department's help in meeting the needs of an important customer and citing Alice's prompt action in particular. I sent one copy of the note to Alice and another to the company president. We all got to be heroes that day.

Subordinates are often overlooked as a networking avenue. If people report to you, they will take you into their confidences only if they think you are doing the same with them. And don't give me that lonely-at-the-top nonsense. That's all it is—nonsense. You don't have to become bedfellows or even best buddies with subordinates. But you're an idiot if you don't make sure you have a mutually beneficial relationship with them. Show them respect and dignity, and they will probably reciprocate.

Many bosses have done themselves in because they took themselves too seriously and let their power go to their head. They manage through intimidation, harassment, and threats, but those tactics don't always work. Faced with unreasonable demands, many people do no more than the least they can get away with, and those who are good enough at office politics can get away with just about anything.

I don't mean to suggest that pressure can't motivate people to work harder, but good managers know how and when to apply pressure. They also know that bullying can actually backfire if you don't know when to turn it on and when to turn it off.

Al Franks was not a good manager. He was a sales manager who got the reputation of being somewhat of a hot dog* because of his habit of grandstanding every sale and taking all the credit

*The pun is most definitely intended, but I didn't dream it up; that's what people thought of him.

no matter who actually closed the order. The salespeople who reported to Al got their commissions, but they resented his downplaying their good efforts.

Neither were they terribly fond of his other habit of restricting their incomes. Whenever any one of them developed his territory to the point where it was producing high commissions, Al would add more salesmen and saleswomen, split the territory, and thereby slice everybody's earnings. Al's boss saw what was happening, but sales were strong, Al was seemingly doing as good a job as anyone could ask of him, and there was no need to fix, as the saying goes, things that weren't broken.

Then a recession hit, and sales didn't fall; they sank straight down, and top management applied intense pressure to stem the tide of red ink. The ball was in Al's court, and he didn't react slowly. Instantly, he sprang a plan B into action. It was brilliant. He told the sales force that everything was their fault and that if they couldn't produce, he would replace them with people who could. Realism? Not exactly.

The truth was that although Al didn't know what else to do, unless business picked up, *everybody's* job would be on the line, his included. He went out of his way to make sure that every order that didn't come through in those dark days was blamed on the alleged incompetence of one salesperson or another.

Still another truth was that although he desperately needed teamwork and extra effort from his people, he forced them in just the opposite direction. Instead of looking for new business, they spent part of their time looking for ways to keep him off their backs and the rest of their time looking for other jobs. They felt isolated, hung out to dry in the winds of change by someone who didn't care in the least for them or their interests.

Unfortunately for Al, the company president was a hands-on manager who liked to see for himself what was going on in the field. With their jobs in jeopardy, several of the salespeople felt that they had nothing to lose by speaking up openly, and their voices were unanimous. Al had the respect of no one and he was soon gone.

What a waste! Al had to go because he acted like a blazing

idiot. Correct that. Al did no acting: He *was* a blazing idiot.

Let your subordinates in on what's going on within the company. Show that you try to see that they are well treated and fairly compensated. Who knows? Some of them may read this book and decide to make themselves more valuable to you. That would be nice, but I can assure you that they won't keep it up if you aren't valuable in return.

There isn't anyone to whom you should *not* be valuable. The individual who can't help you today may be able to do wonders for you tomorrow. The biggest loser in the company may not have much power, but his boss may intentionally seek out weak underlings who aren't a threat. If you don't have occasion to interface with that boss, the way to get a pipeline to him may be to make yourself valuable to the people who report to him.

Having networked sideways and downward, there's no reason why you can't also network upward. Be careful to do nothing that will make your boss feel that he has to fear you; make sure higher level bosses know you and how valuable you can be to them. Use the powerful tools I have already told you about. When you see the top brass coming down the hallway, don't fade into the woodwork. Smile, say hello, and ask how they are doing. If you haven't met them before, find out who they are and the next time you run into them, introduce yourself. They won't bite.

Think of how to be valuable to the upper-echelon types in ways that no one else is using. Do you know any prospective customers the sales manager might call on? Have you read of some new development the chief engineer might like to know about? Do you have a scheme the controller could use to shave some bucks off the latest budget? Don't keep these ideas to yourself—pass them on as ideas these bosses might want to make use of. Just don't be a pest; an ambitious nuisance has no value to anyone.

Don't try to be everything to everybody. You can't do it; nobody can. Neither can you spend so much time making yourself valuable to people that there's no time left to do your work, to make yourself valuable to your boss, or to meet your goals. As far as politics is concerned, the answer is to prioritize as best you can while doing what you can when you can for whomever you can. The way to do this is to:

- be as valuable as possible to the people with whom you must interface to do your job and to increase your value to your boss.
- try to meet and become valuable to others who may be more valuable to you in the future than they are today.
- sort out those individuals who, if you don't stop them, will inundate you with meaningless chitchat and endless boss bashing. Helping them by listening is one thing, but allowing them to dominate your time is quite another. Without offending them, you are going to have to politely get them off your back by claiming to have deadlines to meet, meetings to attend, or errands to run for your boss.

With regard to this last excuse, don't hesitate to use it when it's true. Most people won't react negatively if they have to wait for your assistance because you are doing something your boss has asked you to do. If they see that you can be counted on to get back to them in a reasonable time, they'll understand.

Whatever you do, be courteous and friendly to *all* the people you work with and observant enough to know when to upgrade the attention you pay to any of them.

WHEN ALL ELSE FAILS

You can get hurt if you rush about trying to be valuable to people on nothing more than blind faith in their willingness to reciprocate and be valuable to you in return. Some people will not reciprocate. They'll do nothing *but* take from you, fighting off all pressures to give anything back, no matter how far you have gone to make yourself valuable to them.

They may be ingrates, but don't burden yourself by dwelling on how rotten they are. Look at what you have done for them as investments you have to watch carefully, protect diligently, and ditch unhesitatingly if they show irrefutable evidence of not paying off. If the people with whom you work are not responsive to what you try first, adjust your tactics swiftly, depending on who is involved.

Colleagues who act in a greedy, uncooperative manner can be offered specific trades of certain actions or information you would give them in return for like value provided to you. If that doesn't work, you could threaten to have an uncle from Perth Amboy pay them a visit for the purpose of busting up some of their more fragile body parts, but that would be barbaric.

In my experience, most ornery coworkers will respond quite satisfactorily if you take them aside, firmly say that your aim is mutual gain, not competition, and warn them to cut out the crap or be prepared for open warfare. But don't attack; if your enemies focus on giving you a hard time while you focus on making yourself more valuable than anyone else in the company, the odds are that you will win and they will lose.

Subordinates who won't come around can be similarly handled, on top of whatever additional pressures you can apply in terms of withholding raises or other goodies. If the people who report to you are uncooperative and you are sure of having made genuine offerings of value to them, you may have to give them some lessons in the privileges of rank.

Bosses. If you concentrate on doing well for the company where you work and you find yourself getting dumped on in return, your plan B should be to focus on doing well for your bosses. When all is said and done, what is valuable to a boss may be limited to what *he* wants: *his* security, *his* income, *his* power, and the rest of *his* goals. That's himself he's concerned about—not you, not me, not the company. *Him*. Sure he'd like the company to succeed, but what he really wants is his own success and security. Chances are he views corporate well-being as nothing more than a means to that end.

You may find attitudes such as that too cynical and self-serving to suit your sensibilities, but they are real and they reflect the way a great many bosses operate. Think about it; you will never be hired to do what your colleagues want done, to increase the happiness of the people reporting to you, or to further your own career aims. When you get a job, it's because some manager expects that you will make him happier than anyone else applying for that job.

Later on, in tough, chaotic times, why should that manager keep you instead of someone else? You'll be the one he'll retain if he feels that you're the one who will be most likely to meet his needs. No matter how good an impression you create when you are hired, a continuing ability to meet your boss's needs is the *only* reason you can depend upon for being allowed to hold on to your job.

People in power will want you if they believe that you are necessary to their success. The problem is that if they have big egos, they are apt to take offense at the merest suggestion that they could not meet their goals without you. So tread carefully and convince them that although they could certainly get along by themselves, you can help in a big way—a bigger way than anyone else.

The person you want to help most, however, is you. The way to do that without sucking up is to take advantage of a fact I stated earlier: What you actually do for people is far less important than what they *think* you do for them. If you are good enough at stroking their egos and soothing their fears, they won't care about anything else.

Mel Watson was the first person to point this out to me. Mel carved out a very successful career in spite of being employed by a difficult blowhard named Jim Parr. Jim was as tough as nails on the outside, but he had about as much fortitude on the inside as a bucket of jelly. He was a classic ego case. It was inconceivable to Jim that any of his employees had good ideas or that he ever made any mistakes except to hire those employees. Consequently, he didn't trust them, he wouldn't delegate responsibility to most of them, he badgered them constantly to suck up to him, and he blamed all of them for all of *his* mistakes. All except Mel, that is.

You should have seen Mel operate in a staff meeting. He didn't begin many discussions, preferring instead to start on the sidelines, listen to every word, and watch every reaction. Then, as soon as he was sure what Jim's position was, Mel would chime in to support that position—not by parroting anything the big guy said, but by coming up with an entirely different argument. Mel has long been proud of being able to come up with a reason to justify any point of view, no matter how moronic it is.

Jim was always so wrapped up in himself that it never occurred to him that there was anything strange about Mel's never disagreeing with him. Neither did he question another of Mel's habits, giving what amounts to a speech attacking the enemy whenever someone mentioned a competitor, customer, or former employee Jim didn't like.

Mel didn't grovel or gush, so Jim never suspected that he was being played like a violin. All he heard were ideas he thought were perfectly natural. Since other people's interests were essentially nonexistent to Jim, it also seemed natural to him that in all the years they worked together, Mel never expressed any goals of his own.

Of course Mel had goals. He wanted to make a lot of money. Assessing his talents, however, he long ago concluded that what he was best at was conning people like Jim, so he decided to meet his objectives by being as valuable to Jim as any person could be.

Mel went along with many ideas he disliked, but only because Jim *did* like them. If only the health of the corporation was affected, Mel didn't get concerned about the negative implications of individual decisions made by the venerable Mr. Parr. Mel got *very* concerned, however, when his own plans or his raise were at stake.

Rather than argue in these situations, Mel waited two or three days and then presented what he classified as new information to Jim. Often, he framed it in the guise of a report prepared by someone else who could be blamed for not having gotten the results to Jim earlier. The contents of this report were invariably scrutinized by Mel, orchestrated by Mel, and written or edited by Mel. Considerations and viewpoints that contradicted his way of thinking were never included. By the time the report got to Jim's desk, it was ostensibly a collection of facts, but no conclusions could be reached from it other than those that Mel wanted reached.

Most of the time, it worked. Employees came and employees went, but while Mel kept on making himself valuable, the others kept on fighting Jim or sucking up to him. Eventually, all of them lost or departed. The company is still around, but it is probably not nearly as big or as strong as it might have been had it been run more objectively. In addition to having his ego massaged continuously, however, Jim made several fortunes from the business, so he doesn't care. Neither does Mel; he made a fortune of his own in bonuses from Jim.

But didn't Mel have to do a lot of sucking up in the process? No. He didn't do *any* sucking up. He was not in retreat, he was in control. Furthermore, he wasn't forced to do anything. He did what he did because it was the most direct way to reach his goals. Look at politics as the fact of life that it is, and you'll find nothing sordid about his actions.

Mel didn't get sidetracked, either. He wasn't interested in defeating his boss; his aim was to *use* his boss, and he did that by bringing into play the two most fundamental edicts of politics:

- *Show 'em only what they want to see.*
- *Tell 'em only what they want to hear.*

These commandments provide you with the ultimate means for making people comfortable with you. A weakness for being taken in by what they want to hear and see is the Achilles' heel of people (bosses and others) who have more ego than they know what to do with.

At the first staff meeting I attended after joining a company in Ohio some years ago, my boss asked me if I had any problems. A few matters did have to be cleared up, so I gave him an honest answer. That was the last time I made that mistake. Contrary to what he said, this boss didn't want to hear about problems. Of course he wanted them solved, but that was what he felt he was paying us to do without running to him for help.

The way he saw things, if we brought problems to him, we weren't doing our jobs. Why didn't he say that? He just wasn't a good communicator. We couldn't give him lessons in how to get his points across to us, so we dealt with him as he was. Proving your value to this guy was a matter of talking about *solutions*, the ways in which we successfully handled situations that were problems no more. That's what he wanted to hear, so that's what we told him.

You have no doubt at one time or another seen people praise their boss for what everyone but him knew was a truly lame idea. That's one way of telling a boss what he wants to hear, but if you don't like backing down in the face of stupidity, there's another way to tell hardheaded people what they want to hear, that the good ideas you develop are actually theirs.

I can see it now; you're meeting with your boss and several others to figure out a way to keep key customers informed on a series of new products the company is introducing. You've been down the same road on previous jobs, so you know that a good corporate newsletter is probably the most economical yet effective way to do what has to be done. You also know from experience, however, that if you suggest a newsletter, the boss will spend hours if not days finding fault with it. If the idea were his, on the other hand, the decision would be finalized in minutes.

Here is where careful listening can pay off. Keep a sharp focus on every word he says. Sooner or later he'll come out with something you can twist into sounding like a suggestion that a newsletter is the solution you are looking for. Pounce on it, exclaiming something like, "You've got it!" When he asks what you mean, tell him, "You *are* suggesting that we publish our own newsletter, aren't you?" When he asks again what you mean, say that you think it's a great idea, tell him how it would work, and you may find that he is surprisingly receptive to listening.

I can see you saying to yourself that this is a little hokey.

Maybe you think it's a lot hokey. I don't think that. I mention it because I've done it. A defense electronics business was involved, and a group of us were trying to figure out how to communicate with selected customer groups. Someone in the room suggested that we increase our advertising, and the boss flippantly said it would be cheaper to buy the company that publishes one of the industry trade journals than to pay their advertising rates. I leaped right in with, "You've got it!" and a little while later we were all congratulating him for coming up with the brilliant idea of doing our own publishing in the form of a newsletter.

No, this did not always work. Sometimes I did what Mel taught me to do—watching and listening until I knew what the boss liked and then becoming its champion. At other times, nothing worked. There were times when the boss appreciated nothing but being left alone. I learned to be sensitive to those times, and I suggest that you do the same.

That's when you have to remember Shakespeare's advice about discretion being the better part of valor. There are some fights you can only lose. For those, you have to know when to back off and do what is asked of you by a higher authority. In this regard, as long as keeping a boss happy does not appreciably interfere with your goals, your integrity, your self-respect, or your safety, I say do it. If it has adverse effects on corporate objectives, let the boss worry about them. He's getting paid to do that kind of worrying; are you?

If what is asked of you *would* get in the way of your plans, put your future at risk, or violate your basic rights, you can and should stand your ground. But you won't win unless you have first made certain that you are extremely valuable in your boss's mind. The biggest bullies are often the biggest cowards in disguise. They may not fall over in terror whenever you raise a complaint, but the more valuable they think you are, the more they may worry about your being upset when you protest, and the more likely they will be to act in your favor as long as it doesn't interfere with their own plans or cause them to lose face.

This is the crux of the solution to the third problem I asked you to consider at the beginning of this chapter, which involved a boss with whom you didn't get along and from whom you desperately needed a raise. A raise will come your way only if your relationship with this boss will get better. But that will happen only if *you* change it and make it better. Certainly, your boss won't change it. Considering how badly the two of you get along, she has no reason to make you happy; she might actually prefer you to get so fed up that you'll leave.

But don't take off yet. Take action; it's never too late to try. Begging for a raise isn't necessary; just extend your hand in the spirit of friendship and teamwork. You might even want to be direct and to tell her that you realize that your relationship stinks and that you are going to do everything possible to change it for the better. This is what she will want to hear—that *you* will do all the changing.

Don't ask for anything in return at that point. Just start to become more valuable, and don't make it obvious that you are looking for anything in return. You can't ram trust down anyone's throat. Most people are not idiots; they will not be impressed by shallow compliments or out-and-out toadying. If your intentions are transparent and what you do is seen as patronizing, you might be stopped before you finish, or even before you start.

Make it a sustained effort; be valuable enough long enough, and there's no way you can fail. The only question is how long you can hold out without more money. Do the best you can. Keep it going until you see some signs of less friction or any other improvements in your relationship, and *then* ask for the raise.

If no signs appear within three or four months or if they do appear and you get shot down anyway, move on to a higher-paying job as quickly as possible. That's your plan B, but don't wait to crank it up. Pursue your plans in parallel, and start both of them immediately. You would be wise to allow yourself a few months to find more suitable employment. I don't care if no one is hiring these days; look anyway. You need only one job, and as long as there is more than one available, you still have a chance.

You may never enjoy better working conditions, greater security, or a higher income if all you do is wish hard. If you already have looked for work elsewhere, look harder. Jobs are not buses: They do not come along because you are waiting for them. You have to go find them, and then you have to get them.

Neither will you accomplish anything but aggravate yourself by expecting everyone else to change because your current situation isn't acceptable to you. Maybe your job is fine, your employer is fine, and even your boss is fine, but *you* have to change to bring yourself into sync with reality. Another possibility is that you already *have* changed but you don't know it or don't know how to deal with it.

So before you start looking elsewhere for career enhancement and stability, look in the mirror. If that's too painful, read the next chapter; it's the last.

CHAPTER 7

FORCING THE ACTION

"THEY" ARE NOT TO BLAME

You HAVE seen in Chapters 2 and 3 how to understand and anticipate change. You then saw in Chapters 4 and 5 how to set goals
and make plans that will help you maximize your ability to benefit
from change. Finally, you saw in Chapter 6 how to use politics
to your best advantage in motivating other people to help you
rather than cause changes that will hurt you.

     In spite of this abundance of knowledge, you might dis-
cover one not-so-fine day that things *have* changed, and not for
the better. Any progress you had been making in your career, for
example, may have slowed down or stopped, any success you had
may have vanished, and any security you enjoyed may have
ceased to exist. That would be bad, but even worse would be to
get upset and angry with whomever is to blame for the detour
your career seems to have taken.

     Who could that be? Lots of people. Perhaps the company
that employs you has been sold to corporate raiders who sought
a quick fortune by dismantling everything including your job. Or
maybe the company had a bad year and management was forced

to eliminate raises and to reorganize itself in a way that was not to your liking. If you think either of these is the cause for your problems, spend a few weeks thinking lousy thoughts about your bosses. Better yet, give it a few months. Vent your spleen at how "they" have screwed everything up by virtue of their greed, stupidity, and incompetence.

If that doesn't help, every so often you can get steamed at your coworkers and how "they" sabotaged you by their lack of cooperation and ability. As a last resort, you might as well blow up at your subordinates for giving you no support and then demanding unreasonable rewards in return.

None of these tactics will help in the slightest. Going after scapegoats usually accomplishes nothing but to hide the real culprit: yourself. That's right; if you get derailed by change, the fault is yours alone.

Sure, others may be the reason for changes in the workplace, but they are *never* the reason for those changes having a detrimental effect on your career. Incompetence at the top, for example, may be why your employer went under or got bought out and excessive politics may be why a company is not profitable enough to pay higher salaries, but incompetent bosses cannot possibly be why you have problems, and neither can anyone else.

Did management weld you to your desk so you couldn't leave or look for another job when conditions became intolerable? Was it your peers who blocked your view so you couldn't see what was happening and take corrective actions? Have your subordinates forced you to make the wrong career decisions? Could it be that your enemies confiscated your courage as well as all your plan B strategies?

Nah. Deceive yourself if you like, but don't try to con me. Change created by others can become a problem to you only if *you* weren't ready, willing, or able to change your goals, plans, timetable, or tactics accordingly. If you disagree, you're in for trouble. Instead of thinking with your brain and being honest with yourself, you are either being controlled by your ego or telling yourself only what you want to hear. Either way, you lose.

BLINDSIDING

To be blindsided is to be attacked by someone or something coming at you from a direction other than that in which you are looking. This is precisely why people are surprised by change; they're so wrapped up in their work that they lose sight of their goals.

Being successful requires a major commitment of time and energy. Survival alone often demands nothing less than an all-out effort. Everything happens at a chaotic pace. Your job might be nonstop hectic and you may have to run from one activity, obligation, or responsibility to another on the home front as well. But that's okay, you tell yourself; you are doing what has to be done. And what is that? The usual:

- responding to the pressure of deadlines set by bosses, customers, and everyone else under the sun
- having a grand time being in the thick of the action
- defending yourself against people who seek your job or have the same goals you have and will leap at the first chance to take advantage of you

You may start out with all right intentions, but if you get too caught up in the rat race created by these and other distractions, it's easy to forget why you took your job to begin with. Instead of following your priorities and working toward your goals, you may gradually change your course to the point where most of what you do revolves around someone else's objectives, someone else's priorities, and someone else's schedules. You won't have the time to think about what your goals and plans were, much less figure out what they should be now.

A few years down the road, let's assume that you have met all the company deadlines, achieved the impossible for your bosses, and staved off your foes. Assume further that you have received several raises and promotions. Will that be what you wanted or what you have settled for? The course you're on may

be okay, but it may not be *that* course, the one on which you
started out wanting to be on.

What you want now is probably *not* the same as what you
wanted in the past. Here's why:

• What was at one time exciting and stimulating has a way
of becoming commonplace and boring as you master its intricac-
ies and do it day after day for years. Do anything long enough,
and not only are you likely to get fed up with it, you may thirst
for diversity.

Or maybe you enjoy the pursuit of a goal rather than the goal
itself. Having accomplished what you set out to accomplish, you
may find that the excitement has gone out of your life and that
to be happy, you need new "mountains to climb."

• As you grow and mature, and if your life away from work
expands to include the cycle of events associated with raising a
family, your needs will change and your priorities will change.

• The more experiences you have, the more your horizons
will expand and the more you may become interested in goals
that would have had no way of entering your mind in years past.

In addition to being preoccupied by corporate goals, corporate priorities, and corporate needs and performance requirements, we get blindsided by our own changing interests. And if
a job isn't performing up to our shifting requirements and needs,
we'll hate it, we may find ourselves trying to meet goals we don't
want to meet anymore, and we will become highly susceptible to
the forces of change.

Even if your goals do stay the same as you go up the corporate ladder, your priorities probably won't stand still. If things go
well, the more you accomplish on the job and the better you become at impressing bosses, the higher up you'll go and the more
money you'll make.

There's nothing wrong with that, but if you started in a particular field because you enjoyed the work, you may have to pay
dearly for promotions. As your rank gets loftier, your job will
involve a corresponding increase in administrative responsibilities

such as reading and writing reports, attending meetings, and signing authorizations and other forms of paper shuffling.

Nothing wrong with that, either, but is it how you want to spend your time every day? A great many executives will say no, but then they realize that if they went back to doing what they wanted to do, they couldn't command the fancy salaries they now receive. And they would have a tough time competing with the younger and more easily moldable people the corporate world prefers to hire.

What does the executive in this predicament do? Money may or may not have been an important motivation when he started, but now that he's got it, he doesn't want to give it up. He cringes at the thought of having to trade in the BMW for a used Yugo. More importantly, he may have a family to support and college educations to fund. He may still want what he wanted to begin with, but instead of pursuing it, he decides to hold on to what he has and to make security his highest priority.

Finding themselves in this situation, what many people do is get blindsided by their own fears and draw their wagons in a circle, as the saying goes. Instead of taking the action necessary to get what they really want most, they'll do whatever they can to preserve the status quo. Since an absence of change is impossible to achieve, however, they inevitably fail.

MORE SIGNS

To avoid blindsiding yourself, you have to learn to recognize the conditions under which you are most susceptible to change. On top of the signs and symptoms we reviewed in Chapters 2 and 3, I therefore suggest that you look carefully for the following indications of your own vulnerability:

- **You hate your job.** The more you hate your job, the less you care about it, and the tougher time you'll have coming up with the enthusiasm you'll need to do what you have to do. If you have no zeal for planning, impressing your bosses, networking, and everything else I've been talking about, however, you are about as vulnerable as you can get. If you really hate your job that much, don't just stew about it; make plans to make changes or leave. And don't wait until tomorrow to get started.

• **Your career is not progressing according to plan.** If something did not occur when you wanted it to occur, the only way for you to get back on schedule is to modify one or more goals, strategies, or schedule milestones. When that happens, you are by definition vulnerable to change.

Try to keep your plan out in the open, where you can see it at a glance. If your place of work is not suitable or too public for that, put the plan on a wall at home, where you can check your milestones every day as a constant reminder of your status.

• **You have become sidetracked by thoughts of revenge.** Delivering comeuppance is a meaningful career goal only for assassins or terrorists. Putting bosses in their place won't put bread on your table or provide you with lasting fulfillment. To the contrary, hatred can render you vulnerable by making you forget that your objective is to win, not to force someone else to lose.

A woman I once worked with became obsessed with getting her boss's job by making him look like a jerk. He already was a jerk, so she didn't have much trouble maneuvering him into a position from which he showed his true colors. But when management sought to replace that boss, did they pick my friend? No. She put so much into defeating her boss that she forgot all about impressing his bosses, so her victory was hollow. They saw what she was doing and they thought she might possibly be lacking in team spirit, so they gave the job to someone else, a woman who knew that one does not get ahead in business by demonstrating an expertise as a troublemaker.

- **Your interests have changed.** There's no thunder, no flashes of lightning, and no banner headlines. Out of the blue, all you know is that:

- what you want today is not what you wanted in the past.
- it *is* what you wanted, but then it was your only goal and now it must compete with other interests in your life.
- you don't want it as much as you did when you started, and you won't work as hard or as long to get it as you once thought you would.
- you wanted it and you have it, but it isn't as nice, as satisfying, or as much fun as you thought it would be.
- you wanted it and you have it, but you hate it and now you want out.
- you can't imagine why you wanted it in the first place.

A change of goals is a problem only as long as you are not aware of it. Nobody likes what he or she is doing all of the time, but do you:

- like what you are doing most of the time? More often than not? These are matters for your gut to address, not your brain. If you don't *feel* good about the job you are in, answer no.
- do what you do because you think it's the best way to meet your goals?

If you can't answer these questions in the affirmative, you are doing what you *don't* want to do. This makes you less than fully dedicated, which in turn makes you weak and therefore vulnerable.

Maybe there was a time when you did want to do what you are doing, but that was then and now is now. Maybe you do what you do
for no reason other than that's what you did yesterday and you don't
know what else to do. Force yourself to apply logic. Is your current
job helping you reach some goal? What goal? If you don't have specific answers to both questions, you're vulnerable.

• **Your ego is out of control.** The trickiest aspect
of dealing with ego is keeping your own in check and taking
advantage of the self-confidence it gives you, without losing
it or allowing it to destroy you. Stop yourself *immediately* if
you even for a minute start believing that:

- you are always right and everyone else is always
  wrong.
- people known as "they" are at fault for all your
  problems.
- the only reason you do things is to show that you
  are right and still able to achieve certain goals, or
  that someone else is wrong and less capable than
  you are.
- no one else can be trusted.
- you can't fail.
- the company where you work will fold if you are
  away when an important decision has to be made.
- advice from others isn't worth listening to.
- all matters are of such crucial importance that they
  deserve your personal attention.
- you know all there is to know about a certain subject, so further study in that area would be a waste
  of your time.
- you're so good that you never need a plan B.

I hope you don't believe any of the above. You may be
right quite often. Maybe even usually. But *always*? No way.
I won't believe that unless you prove you can walk on water.

Too difficult? Okay, I'll settle for your being able to eat my wife's horseradish dip without having to drink water.

• **Nobody ever tells you that you're wrong.** How often do the people you work with call you a roaring idiot to your face? How frequently will they say that you are mistaken? That you might be mistaken?

Nobody says things like that? Maybe that's because you have God-like powers and never do anything wrong. A more likely explanation, however, is that you won't tolerate criticism and that people are tired of getting into arguments with you because you won't listen to constructive advice. If you have people reporting to you, they may keep their mouths shut because you have a habit of stomping on them if they find fault with any of your brilliant ideas.

I don't expect you to psychoanalyze yourself, but if you never get any negative feedback, what's probably happening is that your ego has too much influence over you. Rein it in. Force yourself to ask for advice. You certainly don't have to beat on people for giving it to you and you don't even have to take it, but it won't hurt to listen. You may even get some interesting input once in a while.

• **You are playing the national pastime.** Nick Daniels had the smarts and the talent to go all the way but not the fortitude. He got it into his head that survival in the corporate world is a matter of avoiding all risks and planning a future that holds no unwelcome surprises. So he took no chances, consulting with his colleagues on matters affecting them and getting his boss's go-ahead on even the most insignificant activities.

The way he saw the world, if anything went wrong, he could always point out that it wasn't his fault. He did nothing that wasn't approved in advance by his supervisor and supported by an army of peers in meetings that he made sure were well documented by widely distributed minutes.

Nick was absolutely right. Mistakes were made, but

they were never laid on him; he was too good at turning every decision into a consensus that distributed the blame. What he didn't count on was that the same strategy forced him to share the credit for any successes that came along. As a result, he didn't capitalize on what should have been *his* triumphs. And as a result of that, he was bypassed by others who in some instances were less capable as doers but far better than he was at self-promotion.

The same will happen to you if you get too accustomed to playing our national pastime, and I do not mean baseball. That used to be our national pastime, but it isn't anymore. Thirty million tickets are sold annually for major-league baseball alone, but that's nothing compared to the popularity of a game that is practiced every day at every level of every business, government agency, and institutional organization in the country. What is it? It goes by the acronym CYA, which stands for Cover Your . . . well, I had better use *backside* as a euphemism for the third word here.

The premise behind CYA is that "better safe than sorry" doesn't go far enough. A CYA devotee assumes that he or she is better safe than anything. This is the way many people function today. Convinced that even the most infinitesimal risk will result in the most cataclysmic disaster, they pile contingency plan on top of contingency plan, refusing to do anything until they have every imaginable problem covered six ways from Sunday.

Their thinking is not controlled by logic, it's controlled by fear. And their numbers are so large that their warped judgments are having a negative effect on our basic way of life. This is because CYA tells them only what *not* to do, leaving them completely clueless as to what they *should* do.

To avoid failing is not the same as to succeed. If your aim is to climb the corporate ladder, you can avoid failing by staying at the bottom, playing CYA, and not attempting to go up, but no matter how long or how hard you work at it, that strategy won't get you to the top.

All it will get you is bureaucratic red tape, organizational impotence, stagnation, and enough politics to make you nauseous.

CYA is a losing proposition. Its objectives are to prevent change and to avoid risk, but both are impossible goals. You can neither stop nor escape change, and regardless of what you are after, it has a price; you can't get it for nothing and it will never be yours simply because you want it. Part of that price is risk. The more you want—whether it is advancement or rock-solid job security—the more the risk you have to incur.

Beyond that, CYA is dangerous. It's like driving a car without taking your eyes off the rearview mirror. You couldn't do anything without crashing. Neither could you park in the middle of the road; someone would pile into you from behind.

This is exactly what happens to a person obsessed with avoiding all risks. Instead of looking forward and focusing on his goals, he will spend a great deal of time looking over his shoulder for fear that others will attempt to blindside him. He will try to keep things from changing, but he can stop only his own motion. He can't stop anyone else's maneuvering; if all he does is cease moving, someone will eventually push him out of the way or run around him and leave him in the dust.

Of course you should be prudent, but you should also recognize the difference between prudence and paralysis. Job security is as honorable a goal as any other, but you won't achieve it by standing still. You'll get some measure of security only if you become aware of all the changes in your world, and then only if you run as hard as you can and as fast as you can to stay abreast of them as continuously as you can.

SHOWING UP

To take advantage of change, you have to take charge of your career, not merely muddle through it as a casualty of its twists and turns. If your job is *not* enjoyable and *not* helping you satisfy your gut feelings, you can get satisfaction only by making changes of your own. You can change goals, jobs, employers, schedules, or tactics. If one change doesn't get the results you want, you can attempt another and another, individually or in tandem, trying and changing until you find a combination that works. Only you can make these changes. Nobody can make them for you.

New York Times columnist William Safire wrote not long ago about the derivation of the expression "Eighty percent of success is just showing up." According to Mr. Safire, those words came from that brilliant writer and humorist Woody Allen, who first applied them to playwrights. I'm paraphrasing here, but as I remember, Mr. Allen's point was that if you have a great play in you but never write it, the theater that might have featured your fine work may instead be showcasing what other people *do* write. If that happens to be garbage, their success is due only to the fact that they "showed up" and you didn't.

Some people go to work every day, but that doesn't mean they show up. They behave as if they can survive only by whining, complaining, aimlessly hopping around from one job to another, and blaming their troubles on everything and everyone else in sight. This may invoke expressions of sympathy from anyone fool enough to listen, but unless you are entered in a bitching contest, doing nothing but griping about what ails you will accomplish about as much good as spitting on a forest fire.

Showing up doesn't mean putting your job in jeopardy. Neither does it require you to develop superhuman qualities and become aggressive, manipulative, competitive, or gutsy to an extent that you are not. There's a great deal you can do just as you are: by becoming an active participant in your career, not just a spectator.

DISTINGUISH "YOUR" JOB FROM "THEIR" JOB

The first action on your agenda should be to change your employment allegiance. But before you leap to the mistaken conclusion that I'm advising you to get a different job, tell me, who *do* you work for? Answer the question, but *don't* blurt out the name of the company that employs you. That's the way most people would answer. Hoping for rewards that never come, they do more than they should and they give endlessly, but most of them get nothing but a raw deal.

The name I hope you come up with is your own. Work for yourself and no one else. No, I'm not saying you should be self-employed, just that you remember you work because *you* want to benefit from your efforts, not because you feel compelled to do favors for your employers.

Everything you do at work should be directed at moving you closer and closer to meeting your goals. You don't have to be piggish. To the contrary, I've already shown how helping others is one of the most powerful ways to help yourself. Besides, blatantly selfish people needlessly make enemies and I'm sure you don't need any of those.

What you need even less, however, is to spend your life making money for someone else and not getting an adequate return on your time, your energies, your loyalty, your hard work, and your productivity. As a figure of speech, you may say that you work "for" this company or that, but your bottom-line motivation must be more self-centered. Work "at" an organization for as long as doing so is to your advantage. Then move on and work somewhere else. Regardless of where you work, however, toil only "for" yourself and your own priorities.

The question of who you work for is a question of focus. Focus entirely on one company at one address and that's all you think of: the goings-on at that address. You live, eat, and breathe the company line, you put everything you have into doing as good a job as possible, and work your way up the company ladder.

These are fine activities, and if you and your colleagues all do the same, the organization will prosper and its owners may reap a handsome profit. Those employees whose compensation is tied to profitability will also benefit. Will you? I hope so. But the truth is that unless you have a strong contract, the degree to which you benefit from your work may be entirely a function of the degree to which your bosses are fair and equitable.

That degree, I'm sorry to say, is usually quite low. A great many owners and bosses are greedy and unreasonable. They are busy taking care of themselves, and they have neither the interest nor the incentive to take care of you.

Meeting your goals and persuading others to be fair to you is *your* job. The job your employer is paying you to do is "their" job. If you are totally focused on *their* job, you won't be able to do your job. And if you don't do your job, nobody will. To be certain that your job *always* gets done, distinguish it from what your employer wants you to do. Give no less than a 100 percent effort to your employer and show as much loyalty as you feel compelled to show—but only as long as you get what you want in return.

Is your only objective to be the shop foreman where you now work? Please say no. How about vice-president? Say no to that also. President? Still no. These may be fine jobs and worthy of your pursuit, but if you limit yourself to going after them only at one company, you could be totally out in the cold if anything happens to radically change that company. Make sure your career plans are not limited by the confines of any particular organization or its management. Meaningful goals in this regard transcend change by transcending corporate names and boundaries. So whether you want to be CEO or anything else, go for it wherever you can get it, not just at the company where you happen to be working now.

The best way to avoid the career vs. job trap is to recognize the two of them as separate entities. You don't need a job; you need what it does for you. The only purpose for a job is to help you achieve goals such as income level, creative fulfillment, day-to-day work enjoyment, association with others in the same profession, and career advancement. Focus on the end result, and your current job will fall into its proper perspective as your current means to that end.

BE OPPORTUNISTIC

You can react to changes on the job as problems or as opportunities for gain, the difference being that the problems generally hit you right in the head while the opportunities are not so obvious and have to be ferreted out. Those who benefit from adversity are usually thought of as lucky, but in many instances, they are more accurately dubbed opportunists. Very often all the "lucky" ones do is focus on finding ways to gain from each experience instead of wasting all their time grumbling about their losses.

I'm not going to say that a silver lining lies behind each cloud or each change. But I will tell you that nothing is all bad or all good. An exceptionally wise individual once said something to the effect that when life gives you a lemon, the thing to do is make lemonade. Another such person pointed out that every bottle that is half empty is also half full.

In Chapter 6, for example, I described a situation in which a company picnic takes the dark-cloud role. As you may recall, even though attending such a picnic might be offensive, I showed how you can benefit from it if you are able to use the occasion to increase your value to your boss. What I was illustrating there was the process of being opportunistic, forcing the issue, making a change, and finding a way to gain from bad news.

What would you do if your boss made some off-the-wall move that was so moronic that it was beyond stupidity? Would you do nothing but keep quiet for fear of getting bosses mad at you for what they might see as insubordination? Instead of hiding from the situation, I hope you will be opportunistic and take advantage of it. Force a change of your own design by putting in place a plan that may help you change the boss's mind in a way that does not endanger your security. The plan offers you several options:

• Pointing out to the boss how a different approach would let him personally benefit by looking better, smarter, and more valuable to his bosses, customers, stockholders, or anyone else he may want to impress.

• Showing him how the change you recommend would be valuable in terms of efficiency, cost, profitability, or some other reason he would find of interest. Don't generalize. Put forth solid reasons that can be expressed in dollars and cents or some other measurable parameter.

• Giving him an excuse for not having chosen your better idea in the first place. You could say that circumstances have changed since he made his original decision; that what you're telling him is based on new information he didn't have back then; or that some scapegoat withheld, delayed, or misinterpreted that information.

• Presenting him with the opportunity to take credit for the new idea. Do this by telling him about it in private and suggesting that he announce it to everyone else.

Do all this convincingly enough, and not only won't your bosses mind, they will appreciate your loyalty and thank you for it. Do it on a regular basis, and they'll reward you for it.

Janet Martin also got rewarded, but in a different way. Janet lost three high-level jobs, all due to corporate changes that were beyond her ability to control. The first time, her employer was bought out by a competitor and she was out of work for fourteen months. The second time, she worked at a branch office that closed, and it took only four months for her to connect. The difference was not luck, it was opportunism. Janet had learned which jobs to go after, how to apply for them, how to write job application letters that opened doors, and how to interview.

The third time occurred during a recession. That's when Janet decided that she had had enough and would not continue to be bounced in and out of work because the companies that employed her were unstable for one reason or another. While she was trying to get a more secure job, she also went into business for herself as an employment consultant. It didn't take much: $100 or so for business cards and stationery, and there she was—unemployed, yet showing other unemployed persons how to get hired.

They didn't know that she was as out of work as they were, but they didn't care: She knew what she was doing and most of them benefited immensely from her help. After four or five months, she still didn't have a job, but she had stopped looking.

What she did have was so many clients that she couldn't have afforded to take a job if she had found one.

Many successful people are no more intelligent than anyone else. Neither do they necessarily work harder than you or I. Their appearance is probably not noteworthy, either. If you saw them walking down the street, you might not even give them a second glance. Why do they get ahead? They get ahead because they are opportunists: Instead of waiting for success to come to them, they find it everywhere.

Capitalizing on opportunities doesn't have to wait until you're out of work. Everyday situations offer endless possibilities for the sharp-eyed opportunist:

• Your new boss left his door open. You know he likes to lock up because of the important files he keeps in his desk. You also know he's left for the day because you saw him drive off to meet with a customer. Taking things into your own hands, you close and lock his door. That's the right thing to do, but is it all you do? Not if you're an opportunist, it isn't.
First thing the next morning you let him know of your good deed—not in a way that would insult him or make him feel stupid, but by simply saying that you noticed the door was open and that you hope he doesn't mind your having locked up. This is probably not the most exciting advice you've ever received, but it is one of the many simple ways in which you might be able to capitalize on new situations.

• Somebody higher up the ladder than you resigns to go elsewhere. Can you do the job? Do you want it? Perhaps management would give you a shot at it if they knew of your interest. Speak up. Don't demand, but ask for the job. Better yet, don't just ask, make a proposal: Give them some concrete reasons why you would be the best candidate. Maybe you could help the company save money by folding that job into the one you already have.

• Suppose your boss gets sick. Who's going to do his work? It can sit until he gets back; it can sit until he calls in and asks someone to do it; someone else can do it and become a hero; or *you* can do it and become a hero. Taking on authority you don't

have is foolish, but doing work that saves the boss some headaches may be well appreciated.

• The reorganization last week has reduced you to a paper
shuffler. You want out, but while you're looking for greener pastures, you decide to do something productive in the time you have
left. Looking into the mass of forms and documentation systems
that are now an integral part of your work, you come up with
ways that will make your job easier, save a fortune for the company, and make your boss's job easier too.

Good. That's a start, but don't let it end there. Maybe you can
convince the top bosses that you can do the same for other departments. Instead of being hidden away in the lousiest job in obscu-
rity, you might even be able to become the corporate efficiency
expert.

• The impossible has happened and you have made a mon-
strous mistake. Is the earth still rotating on its axis? Good. You
are also still alive. So instead of steaming, stewing, feeling sorry
for yourself, and getting mad at the supposed nogoodnicks who
you think did you in, take advantage of the situation. Be opportunistic. Many experiences repeat themselves in one form or another, and in many situations, only if you can figure out what you
did wrong last time will you be able to determine how to do better
the next time.

PROMOTE YOURSELF

You won't be able to take advantage of most opportunities unless
bosses know how valuable you are or could be. How are they
going to get that knowledge—by virtue of the way your good work
speaks for itself? No. Unless you are working with talking computers or parrots, whatever you do will *not* speak for itself. Neither is there any chance that the great stuff you did today will be
featured on television tonight or written up in tomorrow's newspapers. The people with whom you are competing for promotions
might have some nice words to say about you, but don't count on

it. Sorry, but there isn't anyone else. If you want bosses to get the word about you, you're going to have to get it to them yourself.

A boss may be so busy furthering his own aims, however, that he operates entirely on the basis of what is placed in front of him, not on what he has to dig out. But what's in front of him is likely to be chaos, because there are others who want to get to him with their own messages.

To be noticed and have the effect you want, your message is going to have to be powerful and riveting. It should also be widespread. Write memos, send copies to everyone whenever you have a good idea, volunteer for task-force activities, and don't hesitate to keep touting yourself. People have short memories, and you should make the best use of every occasion to remind your bosses of how valuable you are.

Remember the rest of the world, too. Get yourself in a position to go after outside opportunities, and develop a good reputation throughout your industry. Write articles for trade journals and other media, join civic, political, and trade groups, and become active in them.

Whatever you do in blowing your horn, don't be obvious about it. Look again at the material in Chapter 6 about making a good impression. Self-promotion is most effective if you carefully select which facts to present to people and then let them make up their own minds about your value. And don't try to make yourself look good by making someone else look bad. Doing that can too easily backfire and make you appear valuable only as a back stabber.

Whether you want to get a job or to impress your current boss, "tell 'em only what they want to hear" does not mean that you should give everybody the same story with the same points emphasized. Different people think in different ways and have different priorities. For your message to have the highest possible impact, each person has to be told what he or she will find favorable, which may not be what the next person finds favorable. Before you mouth off about yourself, you had better find out which qualities and accomplishments will impress which people.

RIDING THE TIDE OF TECHNOLOGY

Perhaps the best examples of opportunities offered by change are those that are created every time some major new technology comes along. The computer boom over the last decade or so, for example, has opened up all sorts of ways for people to enjoy themselves, improve their careers, and make a buck by designing, building, selling, programming, servicing, using, or writing manuals for computers, computer parts, computer accessories, printers, cables, or software.

Yet not everybody has benefited from computers. Some people fought them, concerned only that they would lose their jobs if what they did became computerized. They were wrong. Many of them did lose their jobs, but not to a new way of doing things. They lost them to the people who took advantage of change rather than just crying about it.

Some smart executives who weren't hung up on their macho images, for example, taught themselves to use a personal computer. They found that they could finish their memos in less time than it previously took them to write and correct correspondence that was typed by others.

Concerned that this intrusion into their domain might put their jobs at risk, the smarter secretaries kept pace. Some became word-processing specialists and leapfrogged their colleagues who did nothing. Others went even further, moving into desktop publishing, newsletter production, and other specialties that are more diverse, more in demand, and more likely to pay more money.

The same phenomenon has happened in countless other areas in which work that had been done manually is now done better and faster using microprocessor controls. Rather than wiping out jobs, automated manufacturing and design often leads to new classifications of operational and service jobs that offer higher pay for the right skills.

Many people have obtained better and more stable jobs because they were willing to seek out and capitalize on opportunities brought about by technological innovations. Others got left behind. They made the mistake of blindsiding themselves into believing that they were experiencing nothing more than a nightmare that would disappear with a sufficient amount of wishful thinking.

TAKE CHARGE OF YOUR TIME

Time passes by whether we like it or not. We can't set it aside for a rainy day, and we have but a finite amount of it. Furthermore, we are not going to live forever, so we can't afford to take forever to meet our goals. Yet we act as if quite the opposite were true. We all have things to do and problems to solve, but many of us have trouble sticking to our priorities because we're always too busy doing everything else under the sun. We have no time to work on our goals and no time to take advantage of opportunities, much less to find them.

The telephone can be a killer. What do you do when the phone rings? The worst thing you can do is pick it up. I know that's how you use the damn thing, but it's also how you can poorly use your time—particularly if you have important things to do. Surely you know people whose main purpose in life seems to be setting the world's record for insipid yakking. Conversations with them are always the same. They call, you ask, "What's new?" They say, "Nothing," and then go on for the next hour talking about exactly that—nothing. They're oblivious to your lack of interest as long as you throw in an occasional "Mmm" and "Uh-huh."

I say let them find another victim. I have better things to do than listen to their jawboning. So do you. Get an answering machine, get a secretary, or pull the plug out, but don't allow yourself to be distracted or interrupted at the whim of everyone who has nothing better to do than interrupt you. And if you initiate a call, don't be one who is frivolous with time.

The same applies in dealing with others in person. Make it clear that a closed door means you are not to be disturbed and that saying "Excuse me" does not allow anyone to break in on your conversation or your concentration without your permission.

If people stop by your office to pass the time and jabber, tell them you have to tend to some disaster, cut them short, and get back to what you were doing.

Try to avoid being sucked into an endless series of endless meetings. Meetings are the worst time wasters in any job. They can't be avoided entirely, but maybe you can avoid some of them by saying that you are working on a crisis that cannot wait. If you can't make an excuse like that stick, bring some work with you to do while everyone else is babbling. Then make sure not to sit directly across from or next to your boss. To avoid being too obvious, listen every so often and say something every so often. You'll also get some work done every so often, and the meeting won't be a total loss.

Meetings can always use a voice of reason to get things back on track when the subject is changed or when someone (typically a person who has nothing else to do) asks an endless series of moronic questions. Be diplomatic and let that voice be your voice. It's not too hard; simply ask a relevant question about what you think is next on the agenda.

Once you have gotten what you came for, don't hang around if the topic of the moment is drivel you aren't interested in. That is also not too hard; just say you have a problem to take care of and ask if you could leave. Have a plausible answer in mind if someone asks you what the problem is, and vanish.

You're home, away from the office at last. Whether you use the time for work or for personal interests is up to you, but make every second count. When you want to be with family, be with family and don't work. But when you do want to work, go to a prescribed room (or a prescribed corner if that's all you have) and insist that you be left alone until you're finished.

The biggest problem with time management is pressure brought to bear by others. You may want to work on one activity, but your boss, your spouse, your children, and the rest of the world at large will probably have all sorts of different activities in mind for you.

Falling into their clutches is so easy. Your friend David's son is getting married Saturday night. Wouldn't want to miss that.

Then, cousin Annie is having a barbecue. You've always liked her, so there goes Sunday afternoon. You get home from Annie's exhausted, but before you have a chance to sit down, a couple of old friends drop in and you feel obliged to smile, invite them in, and say how happy you are to see them.

You're on a high Monday because as soon as you get home from work, you're going to do some things you've been meaning to get to for weeks. Just as you are about to leave at the end of the day, however, your largest customer calls to tell you he is in town. You of course invite him to dinner and put your own plans on the back burner.

And so it goes, day in, day out. If it isn't David's son's wedding, it's Sara's sister's birthday party or someone else's Sunday brunch instead of Annie's barbecue. And just when you are set to spend Tuesday afternoon on that report you want to finish, some jackass calls a staff meeting. After work, if friends or relatives don't barge in on you, you can always count on your next door neighbor to knock just after you have begun what you had hoped would be a productive evening after a wasteful workday.

These and other demands on your time will always put pressures on you. Those pressures are part of the price we pay for living in a society rather than as hermits. This is not all bad; you wouldn't want to be left alone all day every day. But that doesn't mean you have to surrender control of your time to everyone else. You *can* tell people that you are too busy to meet with them right now; you *can* say you have prior commitments, and you *can* excuse yourself when people call or come to see you unannounced. You can even tell bosses that doing what they want you to do would create big problems for them by preventing you from doing something else.

I am enraged to no end by people who totally disregard the need for priorities and yet unendingly complain about how tired they are, how tough life is, and how they never have the time to do what they want to do. One that comes to mind immediately is a character I'll call Ned the Neat Freak. Ned is consumed with a penchant for cleanliness, the immediate filing of all documents, and the continuous dusting of furniture, floors, and other surfaces. He and I commuted to work together, so I used to stop off at his house on the way to work. He was never on time.

The first day he was late, I waited a few minutes and then rang his bell. He hadn't overslept. He was making the beds, vacuuming, and shining his shoes (*all* his shoes, not just the pair he was wearing that day).

It was the same at work. Ned spent hours stacking his paperwork, putting things away, washing up, and straightening out. All the pencils on his desk were sharpened to the same length. Every day he went through his routines, and every day he would chatter on and on about how much he hated his job. He wanted to get a master's degree so he could command a better job, but he never went for it. He claimed he didn't have the time. I finally suggested that he quit and open up a maid service.

Then there's Dick. He's a software specialist at a manufacturer of electronic instruments. Dick took the job because on paper, it seemed ideal. He would not have to put up with paperwork, personnel problems, or budget worries. The company set up a research lab where he could experiment with advanced designs. His only obligation outside of research was to be what was supposedly a part-time troubleshooter for the company's engineers.

Dick was an expert at getting things done on time and within budgets. Unfortunately, however, he was (and still is) only one man and the company had dozens of engineers. He was in fantastic demand as a problem solver for all of them. He was always in one meeting or another, reviewing one situation or another, as brought to him by one engineer or another. Unless he stayed late or came in on weekends, he had no time for the advanced design aspect of his job.

He reminded his bosses that his intention was not to spend the rest of his life in meetings. They talked about getting him some people to handle the meetings, but their personnel appropriations never came through. He then solved management's staffing problems—by taking a job with another company.

Take a hint from Dick. Controlling your time is not that

hard—all it takes is for you to decide that you'll never make headway toward meeting your priorities if you are always 100 percent wrapped up in what other people want you to do.

Be realistic. Set schedules and milestones, but use them for guides and reminders to be changed as need be. Spend as much time at Sunday barbecues and on the telephone as you like, but keep the emphasis on the *you*. Allocate your time according to your priorities and nothing else. If socializing is at the top of your priority list and your career objectives are all on schedule, fine. But if your milestones on the job are not being met, you had better reconsider how you spend your time after-hours.

How about weekends? If you are too busy during the week, afternoons on Saturday and Sunday are fair game for career matters. If you have to miss an occasional "big" football game or "important" program on the boob tube, that's the penalty you'll have to pay for staying up to date on your career plan milestones.

So you work ten hours (that includes two hours commuting time) every weekday and sleep another six (ten on weekends). You're allowed. And no one's going to fault you for needing two hours a day for meals and wanting another three hours for your family. Add it all up, and you get 135 hours a week. At twenty-four hours a day for the standard-issue seven-day week, your total allocation is *168* hours. Subtract the 135 and you're left with thirty-three—an average of almost five hours a day—to use any way you want. You could be busier than that and have only two hours a day to spare, but don't tell me you have zero hours. I won't believe it!

When you think you have too much work to do and too few hours in which to do it, make a list of each task and how long it will probably take. Block out that time by the day, the week, or the month. By comparing anticipated milestones versus those actually achieved, you will be able to see at a glance where your schedule is tight, where you're going to have to push harder, where you have some slack, and where you may have to make some concessions to reality and revise your plan to make it more workable.

THE MOTHERS OF NECESSITY

If you lost your job, you would immediately begin to look for one or more new sources of income. Your search would be anything but leisurely.

Contrast that with the apathy that tends to smother most of us when we have a steady weekly or monthly paycheck coming in. Mistakenly believing that we are secure, we may decide to do nothing but to play CYA and tolerate whatever types and quantities of crap life dishes out to us. This is when we are most vulnerable.

That's the way George Becker used to be. George had a leisurely approach to life that allowed him to do okay but nothing special. He did what he had to do to get by, but he never pushed himself to increase his income. Opportunities arose from time to time, but to him they all appeared too iffy and too chancy to suit his sensibilities. He was never that comfortable financially, but he was satisfied because his job was safe and his take-home pay was predictable.

Then George's boss sold out to a British company. George kept his job, but the new management took the meat out of it. He was in sales, and many of his big customers were made house accounts, meaning that he would no longer be paid commission on what they bought.

Losing some of his income might not have been a problem a few years earlier, but the change occurred at a bad time for George. His daughter was about to graduate from high school, and college expenses loomed in the not too distant future. Even with financial aid, he had to raise $7,000 or $8,000 dollars in a little over eighteen months. And yet he did it in spite of losing those commissions—with honest money, not a dime of which was borrowed.

George didn't begin printing the stuff. He just turned up the heat: on himself and on every customer or prospective customer he could find. He even took on another sales job nights and on weekends. Calling on hard-to-sell accounts he at one time thought were a waste of his time, he found that he was a better salesman than he had thought he was. He also discovered that he could work harder than he thought possible, and yet he was achieving so much that instead of being tired at the end of the day, he was excited, all pumped up and ready for more.

The following year, the engine blew out on his car. Logic told him he couldn't afford a new engine, much less a new car. But he couldn't do anything without wheels, so he went shopping. Walking into a showroom one day, he saw a bright red convertible. It was loaded with all kinds of options he didn't need and it cost far more than he had in his budget, so of course he bought it. His brain didn't like the idea, but his gut was all for it and that's why he did it. And guess what? His income rose to meet his needs. He had to work harder, get into a different business, and change jobs to make it happen, but he did it *because he motivated himself to do it*.

No, this is *not* another one of those you-can-do-whatever-you-put-your-mind-to-doing lectures. Had he needed $50,000 or $100,000, maybe George would have failed, but who knows? Maybe he would have found a way to get ten times that much. All I know for sure was that he wound up raising a lot more than he would have raised had he not tried at all.

Perhaps you've heard that one has to spend money to make money. In some cases that's true, but I prefer to say that one has to invest something to make money. That something may also be money, but it doesn't have to be. It can also be your time, your energy, or your reputation.

Sometimes, you don't have to spend anything. You may only have to *risk* something, to take a gamble. This may require more guts than you have previously been able to find, but getting the most out of life requires you to stick your neck out every so often. To avoid getting your head chopped off in the process, you don't need guts, you need a good plan B. To get yourself off dead center and moving toward the next milestone, however, you need action. Action without the backup plan would be crazy, but a backup plan is useless if the only thing it motivates you to do is to play CYA.

George Becker turned himself around because he figured out

how to take risks. The more ambitious his goals were, the more risk he had to incur and the more courage he was required to invest. He spent years chugging along at half speed, meeting his needs and therefore having no incentive to do any more. Then his needs changed and he was forced to change accordingly. He got what he needed, but he did it the hard way—wasting an awful lot of years when he could have been doing it all along but wasn't.

How about you? Can you be motivated to be bolder and more aggressive than you've ever been before? Of course you can if something happens to terrorize you, but what if a disaster never occurs? Can you jump-start yourself, or are you doomed to the mediocrity of playing it safe the rest of your life?

While invention may have one mother (necessity), it has *two* grandmothers: fear and pressure. It's hard to directly force yourself to become afraid of something, but you may be able to create fear indirectly by imposing tons of pressure on yourself.

One way to do this is to take on so much work that you load up your schedule, filling all of your time and then some. The fear of missing deadlines will eventually force you to take control of your time, set priorities, and make sure that your most important obligations are met. If in fact you keep the pressure on, you will find that you get a lot more accomplished than you previously would have thought was possible. This is what George Becker did.

What you have to do is continuously challenge yourself and stretch your efforts beyond the point of what is easy to do. Certainly you don't want to stretch so much that you break, so ease into it. Take on more and more, push yourself more and more, and do more and more. To put some impetus behind you, buy something you want. Don't wait until you save up the money; do it now. Then you won't have any choice: you'll have to force yourself to budget the money or to work harder and earn the money.

If you restrict your initial purchase to something you can find the funds for within a few days or weeks, the penalty for your being so adventurous will be minimal. At that point, however, ask yourself what else you might want. Stretch yourself even further. Get yourself accustomed to the pressure and to making a plan. Your goal in that plan is how much money you need, and your

method of accomplishment is how you will get that money between budget rearrangements and additional earnings.

This is not fiction. It's all true. Instead of saving to accumulate the cash necessary to buy what he wanted, George learned
that he did much better by reversing the procedure and taking
on specific obligations that forced him to extend himself to the
limit.

Reckless? Not at all—I said *to* the limit, not past it. He had
last-resort contingency plans to mortgage his house if necessary
to finance his daughter's education. As far as the convertible was
concerned, he asked himself, What's the penalty? Concluding
that the worst that could happen would be to have the car repos-
sessed, he took it. He kept it, too.

With the right plan and realistic goals, you will find that the
more you have to do, the more you can do and the more you *will*
do. This is not a pitch to change your attitude; if all you have is
a positive attitude, you will not succeed. *Positive attitudes aren't
worth two cents unless they are accompanied by positive actions.*

If this sounds undoable, you haven't tried it. All it takes is
a willingness to push yourself until you find your real limits, not
just those with which you are comfortable at your laziest.

IT'S NEVER TOO LATE

As bad as it is having your job go sour, it's worse to have it taken
away. I hope that never happens to you, but let's assume for the
purpose of discussion that it does and that you keep your wits,
refusing to feel sorry for yourself *or* to waste time seeking out
scapegoats. What do you do to get back on the right track?

What you do is to get started from wherever you are. It's
never too late to set employment goals or to develop contingency
plans of the sort I described in Chapter 5. And although it's hard
to make friends at a company where you no longer work, it's
never too late to make use of business contacts and the friends
you do have. They can serve as references and as lookouts for
job openings.

It's also never too late to learn the basic concepts of copy-writing in the direct-mail advertising arena. These are the concepts you should be using when you send résumés or job-application letters to prospective employers. And until you meet someone who might agree to make you an offer, it's never too late to take another look at Chapter 6: Telling people what they want to hear and convincing them of your value is crucial to successful job interviews.

Equally crucial is your willingness to admit your ignorance in these matters. You may be a fine rocket scientist, but you probably don't know beans about selling yourself, and self-promotion is the key to getting hired.

YOUR MOVE

I know that being told to take responsibility for their careers isn't what some people want to hear. Still others may have a hard time believing that the means for stabilizing their careers can be found by reading a book that costs only a few dollars. They'd be much more comfortable with my suggestions if I were to trot out an 800 number and offer a package of grossly overpriced subliminal cassette tapes and motivational seminars, each purported to feature a shovelful of success secrets available from no other source.

As an added incentive, I would throw in a set of dishwasher-safe, stainless-steel steak knives guaranteed to last a lifetime. And to crush the last vestiges of sales resistance, I would promise to accept all major credit cards.

Magic solutions and hype, however, are not my game. Neither is taking my readers for a ride. I have no seminars, no tapes, no knives, and not even a toll-free telephone number. You need that stuff about as much as a camel needs a third hump. Besides, I long ago decided to wait until writing my *next* book before divulging the secrets of the universe.

You can also wait. Someone else may come along and take care of change for you. Perhaps a line is now forming of people who are fighting amongst themselves for the honor of bailing you out. But in case you find that others are too busy solving their own problems to worry about yours, don't hold your breath. There is a better solution.

What is it? Simple. Instead of covering your you-know-what, you should get it in gear. Not tomorrow. *Now*. Whether you want to create, prevent, or undo the effects of change, doing it yourself is the only way that works. Regardless of how much or how little influence you have over other people, you have total control over the extent to which the changes they cause can impede or advance your career. You also have complete freedom in deciding whether, when, and how to create other changes of your own.

The fact is that unless you actually *do* something about change, you are relying on dumb luck to see you through. Sometimes that works, but more often than not it results in an abundance of dumb accompanied by a scarcity of luck.